Reviews

"The Lord Jesus came, not only to give us eternal life in Heaven, but also abundant life here on earth (John 10:10) – that we might thrive! In this book, Linda's immensely personal approach makes you feel as though she is sitting right beside you, encouraging you through every step. Rising far above mere explanations, her inclusion of life experiences, poignant quotes, and practical workspaces provide what every woman needs to thrive for the Lord."

– **Kevin J Currell,** Principal of Victoria Baptist Bible College; Evangelist; Author of *Essential Bible Insights: A Study of Manners & Customs of Bible Times*

"*Thrive to Make a Difference* is a delightful book of practical and spiritual helps for today's Christian woman. Linda's engaging and encouraging insight is a must-read!"

– **Melanie Smith,** Sword of the Lord Publications

"A fascinating journey of a woman seeking a higher purpose amidst the doldrums and frustrations of daily life. This extremely practical book holds the key to revolutionize every woman's deepest desire for divine approval of a job well done."

– **Richard Hester,** Founding Pastor of Faith Baptist Church, Sydney; Principal Emeritus of Sydney Bible Baptist College; Author of *Cast Your Bread, New Testament Bible History Handbook* and *Old Testament Bible History*

"We highly recommend *Thrive to Make a Difference* to any woman who wants to achieve her unique purpose and make a difference in this world. There are many encouraging truths in this book, and Linda has a wonderfully engaging way of including stories and illustrations from her own life. Spiritually edifying topics include roles, priorities and setting habits, as you assess your life and create your own Thrive Plan."

– **Keith Piper,** Pastor of Liberty Baptist Church, Sydney; Author of *Answers Book, Understanding Book, Established in the Faith* and *Jesus Christ's Life in Pictures*

– **Tania Piper,** Children's Ministry Leader at Liberty Baptist Church, Sydney; Religious Education Teacher; Author of *To You Alone*

A Christ-centered approach to intentional living

THRIVE

TO MAKE A DIFFERENCE

Learn how to identify and live out your God-given priorities through your personal Thrive Plan, to help you focus on what matters most every day.

LINDA KARKAFI

WESTBOW
PRESS®
A DIVISION OF THOMAS NELSON
& ZONDERVAN

WestBow Press books may be ordered through booksellers or by contacting:

WestBow Press
A Division of Thomas Nelson & Zondervan
1663 Liberty Drive
Bloomington, IN 47403
www.westbowpress.com
844-714-3454

www.thrivetomakeadifference.com
Instagram & Facebook: @thrivetomakeadifference

Scripture taken from the King James Version of the Bible.

ISBN: 978-1-6642-4912-7 (sc)
ISBN: 978-1-6642-4914-1 (hc)
ISBN: 978-1-6642-4913-4 (e)

Library of Congress Control Number: 2021922282

Print information available on the last page.

WestBow Press rev. date: 02/08/2022

Learn how to identify your
God-given priorities through
your personal Thrive Plan.

A Christ-centered approach
to help you focus on what
matters most every day.

Dedication

To my first love,

Jesus Christ.

To my cherished

husband and best friend,

George.

To my beloved children—

Bethany Joy,

Samuel Alexander,

and Marie-Therese.

Contents

PART ONE: THRIVE WITH PERSPECTIVE

1. You Can Thrive 3
2. The Perfect Foundation 13
3. It's Time to Dream 41
4. We All Need a Vision 53

PART TWO: THRIVE WITH A PLAN

5. A Life with Purpose 71
6. Your God-given Priorities 79
7. Setting Your Thrive Goals 89
8. Achieving Your Goals 111

PART THREE: THRIVE WITH PASSION

9. Planning for Victory 127
10. Visualize Success 139
11. Thriving as a Way of Life 145
12. It's Time to Thrive 163

Daily Devotions 170
The Gift of Eternal Life 210
Acknowledgments 217
Notes 219

Part One

You know the days. The laundry is out of control. Dishes have piled up. Your children need you. Your work deadline is looming. You're feeling overwhelmed and tired. Pulled in so many directions, you wish you could just hit pause for a moment and rest.

Welcome to the world of womanhood. Where the work never finishes, life never pauses, and the constant call for your attention is relentless. You crash at the end of the day, only to wake up in the morning to do it all again.

Friend, I'm here to tell you that life can be so much better. You don't have to feel overwhelmed and exhausted all the time. Nor do you have to feel guilty or full of regret. It is actually possible to rise above the daily grind and find

satisfaction and purpose like never before. You can feel like a great mother, a great wife, a great friend.

You can make a difference in this world. Sister, you can thrive. My commitment to you is to help you get there.

In the coming pages I'm going to personally take you on a journey where you can discover what it means to thrive. I want to help you become clear about your priorities and on track to achieving your life goals. I am confident that through prayer, God's Word, intentionality and discipline, you will be well on your way to thriving in your life and making a difference for eternity. I'm honored that you would join me on this journey.

CHAPTER 1

You Can Thrive

> *Now unto him that is able to do exceeding*
> *abundantly above all that we ask or think,*
> *according to the power that worketh in us*
> *(Ephesians 3:20).*

One of the things I've found myself grappling with, as a wife and mother of three young children, is that the work never ends. Like, never. The weekend promises rest and relaxation, yet even on those days "off" the housework continues to pile up (are you nodding?). I have constantly strived to be one step ahead and not feeling like I'm always playing catch-up. To feel a sense of achievement and purpose in the seemingly mundane moments of life. I confess that I have often felt overwhelmed.

As women, we play a critical role in the lives of others— whether our husband, children, friends, relatives or colleagues. As we nurture and love the people God has given us with everything that is in us, we give, give, give, and give some more until we find ourselves depleted.

But what if I told you that it didn't have to be this way? What if I told you that there is a better way to live?

I'm not suggesting that you ditch the dishes or give up on duty. What I am suggesting is that you take a step back and seek a fresh perspective on your life. Something, perhaps, that you haven't had the luxury to do amid the constant hustle, week in and week out. Today I want to give you the permission to pause and carve out some space for reflection.

I believe that reflection is not common practice among Christian women today. We tend to forge ahead in life, putting all our energy into our daily routines. We become so reactive to the needs of others that we lose touch with why we are doing what we're doing and how we ought to be going about it. We start to totally miss Jesus in it all and start "doing life" our own way. This then leads to frustration, fatigue, a lack of motivation and, potentially, even feelings of resentment ("Why can't someone else scrub this bathtub?!"). We start turning to things or people to fulfill our lack of contentment. A shopping fix, gossip-fest, holiday or social media—we look to these things to escape the mundane reality of our own lives. We look around us and can't seem to avoid the images of beautiful women in picture-perfect homes, living their best life yet—the kind that seems so out of reach to us.

Sister, it was never meant to be this way. The cross is meant to lead us to a life of joy and liberty. A life with purpose, contentment, and hope. I'd like to suggest that as a generation we have lost our way. But there is hope. The way back is not too far out of reach.

God's Word is our road map, and it reveals the perfect path to finding satisfaction in our earthly lives. By taking a step back from where you are standing today and allowing Jesus to reveal to you His vision for your life, you can find the remedy to feelings of frustration and discontent which arise from time to time.

God has a purpose for your life, and the amazing thing about it is that only you can accomplish it. You have been gifted with a unique set of talents, experiences, and desires—together, they are what makes you so special. And your loving Creator, God Himself, is preparing a future for you that only you can bring to fruition.

I'm always amazed to see women around the world doing incredible things for God's kingdom—things I could only dream of accomplishing. But in the same way, the Lord has given me specific abilities in areas that other women find daunting. The qualities that make me special were entrusted to me by God to accomplish His purpose for my life here on earth. We all have a special place in this world. We all have the opportunity to shine the light of Jesus and play our role in the body of Christ. We simply need to create the space in our life where we can seek the Lord for His direction.

Have you ever wondered why some women are more intentional in their lives than others? Why some women are achieving great things for God's kingdom, while others seem to be continually struggling with the same spiritual battles as before? I am confident that women who are thriving in their walk with Jesus have one thing in common—they regularly take time out with Jesus and allow Him to define their life priorities.

Do you want to be that kind of woman? Well, precious sister, I have written this book to support you. My heart yearns to see you rise up above the daily grind and gain a fresh perspective of what God wants to do in your life. I want this for you, and I want this for countless other women who feel overwhelmed and in need of hope.

In the pages of this book, I want to walk you through a process I have developed that will help you gain perspective in your life. This process is Christ-centered and rooted in the Word of God.

One simple step at a time, I will walk you through exercises that are designed to help you set the foundation and structure for your life plan—which I call your Thrive Plan.

Your Thrive Plan will help you live a more intentional and proactive life for Christ. It will help ensure that the daily decisions you make about what to do with your time are helping you work toward your life vision and God-given priorities. You will start with your Christ-led dream and will end with a practical plan that you can start living out immediately.

Your Thrive Plan will form the basis of how you invest your time, how you make decisions about what to focus on each month, and how you engage with your family, friends, church, workplace, and community.

The process is simple, but it will only work if you play an active role in it. One of the most important actions you will take throughout this Thrive Journey is to pray. Then you will take time out to listen to God as you read the Scriptures and seek to know God's purpose for your life. I'm afraid there simply are no shortcuts when it comes to discerning God's purpose and priorities for your life.

What has this Thrive Process done in my life? It has helped me develop a strong sense of focus and fulfillment. My career background is in strategic consulting, so planning is second nature to me. I enjoy developing strategies for leaders and helping them achieve their business vision and priorities. I emphasize the importance of each individual in an organization understanding what their role is and how it fits into the overall vision of the organization.

Yet personally I often struggled to see how I was living out God's purpose for me in the daily, seemingly mundane, duties of life. There were certain things I wanted to achieve or things

I wanted to focus on, yet as each week passed, I felt like the urgent matters demanding my time were squeezing out the less urgent, but no less important, things I needed to pursue.

Then when I set aside time with the Lord to prayerfully consider what He wanted me to focus on and translated these priorities into measurable actions, I really started to experience a wonderful feeling of

I want to help you thrive. Not survive another week. Not strive to do better. But by the grace of God, to thrive and succeed in the life God has called you to live.

accomplishment that brought joy and fulfillment in my heart. I am sure you have heard the age-old quote, "If you don't plan your life, someone else will do it for you." Well, I don't know about you, but I want the Lord to be the One planning my life!

My dream is to see hundreds and thousands of Christian women find perspective in the midst of the chaos of life, to nurture a generation of women who are filled with the peace of God and empowered to be anything God calls them to be. I truly believe that with intentional Christ-centered planning and executional rigor, we can raise up a generation of women who are reaching new heights for the glory of God.

Sister, I want to help you thrive. Not survive another week. Not strive to do better. But by the grace of God, to thrive and succeed in the life God has called you to live. I want to help you achieve your unique purpose on this earth so that you can make a real difference in your family, church, friendships, workplace, community, country, and the world.

So, let's start the journey with you today and who knows who you will inspire as you "thrive to make a difference in this world."

God bless you!

Whatsoever thy hand
findeth to do, do it with thy
might (Ecclesiastes 9:10).

CHAPTER 2

The Perfect Foundation

My husband is an engineer and builder. Each new building project starts in the same way. They dig deep and excavate the land. Then they pour tons of concrete as they form the foundation of the building. Without the digging and pouring, the building will not stand firm on a strong foundation. That is precisely what this part of the Thrive Journey is all about.

Before we seek to thrive for Christ, we need to ensure that the foundation we are building on is immovable and unshakable (Matthew 7:24–28). The Lord Himself is the Creator of all life, the Author of faith, the Alpha and Omega, the Beginning and the End. He alone can reach into our hearts and save our souls. He alone can implant abilities, desires and passions that are perfectly aligned to His plan for our lives. While God has a unique purpose for your life, you can only begin to understand it when you know Him on a personal level.

Then what is our role in the planning process, you ask? We need to seek Jesus. We need to pray. We need to trust Him. Then we need to take a step of faith. Keeping our Savior at the foundation, the center, and looped all around our plans is the only way we can truly make the kind of difference in this world that will count for eternity.

> Keeping our Savior at the foundation, the center, and looped all around our plans is the only way we can truly make the kind of difference in this world that will count for eternity.

May I take a moment to remind you that your life was not a coincidence? You did not come about through a random act of science. God, the Maker of the universe, created you. Right there in your mother's womb, He knew you and loved you. He planned out a beautiful life for you. With a purpose and plan that only you could fulfill. You are loved.

Jeremiah 31:3 says, "The LORD hath appeared of old unto me, saying, Yea, I have loved thee with an everlasting love: therefore with lovingkindness have I drawn thee."

Sometimes it is hard to comprehend Jesus, the Bible, and the cross. It may feel like a nice religious story from ancient days, but I want to share with you today that it is not just a story. Jesus came and declared openly that He is the Way, the Truth, and the Life, and that no one can go to the Father but through Him (John 14:6). There is an exclusive path to God, and that's through Jesus Christ alone.

No one can make a valid claim to be perfect. We all know that we live daily with the tendency to sin. We all make mistakes. We are riddled with imperfection. But Christ, who was perfect, blameless, and sinless, chose to deal with our imperfection by taking the punishment for our sins. It's impossible to comprehend why Jesus would die for our sins and why He had to die to give us life. But once you embrace this truth and invite Jesus into your life, then—and only then—will you be free from the shame of your sin and experience true forgiveness and peace in your life.

Truth be told, before you can thrive for Christ, you need to be *in Christ*. Before you can seek God's direction for your life, you need to personally know the Savior. He has a wonderful plan for your life and desires to reveal it to you. If you have never entered into a personal relationship with Jesus Christ, I ask that you consider your eternal destiny. Please refer to the section at the end of this book titled "The Gift of Eternal Life" for more context.

The power of God's love is so amazing that thousands of years after His resurrection, Jesus is still changing lives today. Indeed, there is a living God who seeks to know you personally. He loves you and wants to give you a brand new life today. I pray that you will open your heart and allow God to speak to you personally.[1]

MY STORY

I was blessed to be raised by loving Christian parents who took my brother and me to church each Sunday. We attended Sunday school and youth group and stored up many beautiful memories. When I was nine years old, I asked Jesus to be my Savior and committed my life to Him. It was the most important decision I ever made. I immediately felt a change in my life, even to the point that the next day I took my Bible to school and tried to share with my friend how she should love her brother and not fight with him (I sure hope I was taking my own advice). As the years went by, I grew to love Jesus more and more. When I turned 18, I got baptized and started to teach my first children's Bible class. Over the years as I have walked with the Lord, sat at His feet, and trusted Him through several seasons of life, I can honestly say that life without Christ is just not worth living. He has shown me His faithfulness, kindness, love and mercy in so many ways. I truly can't stop praising Him for who He is and all that He has done in my life. So when I say that you need to be in Christ to live for Christ, I'm sharing with you from my own personal experience.

If you are in Christ, then sister, let's take this journey together. Let's allow the Lord to search us and build us from the ground up. And if you're still a little unsure about this whole gospel thing, read on; blessings are awaiting you.

IT'S TIME TO TAKE STOCK

At the end of each school semester, our children come to us with their school report cards. It's an exciting and important time when we get to see the results of their hard work. It's also a great way to assess their strengths and the areas where improvement is required. Then on the basis of the report, we can clearly plan a way forward to help nurture and support them to reach their full potential.

Let's take a few moments now to create our own spiritual report card by examining the state of our heart. Allow me to ask you a few questions. Firstly, how is your walk with the Lord right now? Would the word "intimate" come to mind or "strong" or perhaps "distant" or "lukewarm"? Would you describe your relationship with Jesus as a *thriving* relationship?

What about your prayer life? Is prayer a daily habit in your life that you have come to enjoy and rely upon? Or is prayer more of a hit-or-miss strategy, something that you know is important, but you struggle to commit to? Do you pray strategically and proactively? Or do your prayers tend to be reactive and mostly about what you are going through right now? What about your devotional life? Are you carving out quality time to spend with Jesus each day? Do you honestly look forward to spending time with Him and being guided by His Spirit? Could you say that you are placing Jesus first in your life each day?

The reality is that unless our lives are full to the brim

with the presence, power, and perspective of God, then we cannot live a thriving life. It is vital that we nourish our souls daily and allow God's Word to direct us. More than ever, we need to spend quality time with Jesus each day, that we may discern His promptings and live our lives in a way that truly honors Him.

The truth is, the only way we can thrive in any circumstance of life is by making Jesus our number-one priority. When we spend time with the Lord daily, we have the opportunity to renew our mind and receive grace to face each challenge in a way that glorifies Him. It is the only way we can have a fruitful, satisfying life, regardless of what we are facing or the season we are living through.

A FRUITFUL SEASON

I found the season of singleness to be a very busy and fruitful one in my life. One of my cherished memories was leading our church Sunday school program. The Lord placed on my heart such a deep burden for the kids of our church and a desire to help them nurture a close walk with Jesus at a young age. When I had my own children, I felt triple-blessed to be part of their spiritual journey and to be with Bethany and Samuel, our two eldest kids, when they committed their lives to Christ.

Over the years I was blessed to watch my Sunday school students grow up and enter their chosen vocations. From nurses and engineers to teachers and builders. It's incredible to see how these precious little children have grown to be men and women, many of whom are still in church to this day and have a strong desire to serve the Lord.

While I'm on this topic, a quick message to any person reading this book whom I had the privilege to teach in Sunday school. My heart still yearns to know that you love Jesus. My favorite song to sing with you included the words "Build your life on the Lord Jesus Christ and the blessings will come down—the blessings will come down as the prayers go up."[2] Tears would often fill my eyes as we sang this song together, as it perfectly captured the Lord's heart for you and the desire He placed in my heart for your life. I don't know where life has taken you, but I just want to say to you one more time—Jesus loves you, He knows your name, and He will never forsake you. Trust in Him, believe His Word, obey His commandments, and you will be well acquainted with His perfect will for your life. You can shine so bright—in a way that no one else can—because you are loved. And you are SO special.

During the time when I was leading the children's ministry in my church, I also happened to be working full-time and studying for a master of business degree. It was hectic to say the least, but the Lord challenged me to put first things first, regardless of the pressure I was feeling. I made a commitment to honor the Lord and start each day with Him, no matter what. This decision was precisely what enabled me to complete my postgraduate degree and be fruitful in ministry. The Lord showed me, day by day, that with Him, and with Him alone, I could make it. I found that as I continued to attend all church meetings and invest my time in the ministry, the time I had left to study was more efficient and effective than it had ever been before. I felt God's presence and help during that time in my life, and as a result I can testify that it was such a fulfilling journey.

In Jeremiah 15:16 the prophet Jeremiah says, "Thy words were found, and I did eat them; and thy word was unto me the joy and rejoicing of mine heart: for I am called by thy name, O Lord God of hosts."

Notice how this verse says, "Thy words were found." It's a reminder to us that we need to search God's Word. We literally need to open the Scripture and consume it; otherwise, we are choosing to forfeit the "joy and rejoicing" that God has prepared for us each day.

Do you want to know the heart of God for your life? Are you searching the Scriptures daily? You have to start with His written Word; that is where the Thrive Journey must begin.

STARTING WITH A BLANK CANVAS

I need to make a confession right here and now. I love stationery. For all you stationery lovers out there, you know what I am talking about. For the rest of you, please bear with me. While women get excited to start the year with a new handbag or perhaps the latest phone, I am thrilled to purchase a new diary (I know, it's embarrassing). I get so much delight as I turn to the first new page of my diary and dream of what the year ahead will bring.

I believe the Lord also enjoys new seasons. In fact, He specializes in new beginnings. So today, we're going to allow the Lord to do something new in our hearts. I want you to ask God to examine your heart today. Yes, you need to dig deep and eradicate any sin you may be harboring in your life. Why so brutal, you ask? Because sin lurking below the surface of our lives will hinder us from achieving God's purpose, and that's what we're here for, right? Like beginning a fresh new page in a diary or on a beautiful blank canvas, let's allow the Lord to start a fresh new work in our lives.

Allow me to ask you some personal questions. Are you daily confessing your sins? Are you seeking God's power to help you overcome habitual sin in your life? If you are feeling a lack of peace, joy or passion to do what God has called you to do—it may be that you are harboring sin in your heart. To be close to the heart of God, we need to eliminate anything that is lingering between us and our Heavenly Father. Only when we are cleansed by Christ's forgiveness can we enjoy a clear conscience and better discern His will for our lives.

David cries out to the Lord in Psalm 139:23–24. He says, "Search me, O God, and know my heart: try me, and know my thoughts: And see if there be any wicked way in me, and lead me in the way everlasting." In these verses we see that repentance and seeking to be right before the Lord is something "intentional." We need to make a habit of coming before the throne of God and asking Him to examine us. When the Holy Spirit reveals to us areas of sin in our lives, or sins of omission (things we should do and are not doing), we can then and there receive cleansing. And truly it is the best feeling in the world when you have a clear conscience before God.

A verse that I can't possibly leave out is the following: "If we confess our sins, he is faithful and just to forgive us our sins, and to cleanse us from all unrighteousness" (1 John 1:9). We need to make sure we are allowing the Lord to cleanse us from our sinful thoughts and actions on a daily basis. Through daily confession and repentance, we can enjoy the beauty of staying in close fellowship with Jesus. We can enjoy a blank canvas on which Jesus can paint a wonderful story for our lives.

IS ANYTHING WEIGHING YOU DOWN?

I'll never forget the last few weeks of each of my three pregnancies. I waddled from side to side as I felt the intense weight of my beautiful, big babies resting comfortably within. As each big day approached, I was sure they were going to come early. But they never did. In fact, my first child, Bethany Joy, was ten days overdue—and even then, I still had to be induced. To say I was uncomfortable is an understatement. I tried everything to bring on that labor—walking around the block, special exercises—you name it, I tried it. But the Lord had the perfect day in mind, and His timing was right. It was a day I will cherish forever.

After 36 hours of pre-labor, we ended up preparing for an unplanned C-section. As I waited to enter, George prayed with me. I felt peace. I was so ready to meet my baby. After about 30 minutes it was time, and I heard her first cry. The doctor announced, "It's a girl!" and I felt my heart would burst for joy. They laid her on my chest, and she took my breath away. I can never forget the moment she opened her beautiful brown eyes; it was love at first sight, and my heart melted. She was simply perfect and absolutely worth the wait. Bethany Joy lived up to her name the day she was born, bringing so much joy to our hearts and to our entire family.

Following the delivery, the most notable change I felt in my body was the weight that had been lifted, both physically and emotionally. I felt lighter and much more comfortable in my own skin.

Bearing the weight of my daughter for nine months was, of course, well worth every moment; however, there are other weights that we choose to bear in our lives that are not at all worthwhile. In fact, some weights that we carry are an absolute waste of our time and energy. Harboring unnecessary weights in our lives only brings us down and holds us back from living for Christ. Now I know this is a heavy topic, but please stay with me. I deeply desire for all women to feel liberated and free to pursue their God-given dreams and priorities—and that includes you, sweet sister. Here I want you to deal with any stumbling blocks in your life that are causing your foundation to be less than stable.

Perhaps the things that are weighing you down are not necessarily sinful in and of themselves, but they are distracting you and deterring you from fully surrendering your life to Jesus. I want you to take a few minutes now to pray and surrender anything God has brought to your attention. Simply confess any sin in your life. Surrender your heart afresh to Jesus. Ask Him to clear your way as you start this exciting journey. Then, in the space provided, write down the date of your prayer and briefly what you prayed about.

_____

_____

_____

_____

_____

_____

TIME TO PRAY

Prayer plays such an important role in my life. I have come to depend on speaking to the Lord each morning, throughout the day, and into the evening. I am telling you, sister, I can't imagine my life without prayer. Through prayer I feel my burdens lifted and my soul refreshed. Nothing is passive about prayer. The more you intentionally speak to your Savior, the more you will be filled with His peace, perspective, and purpose.

Before moving on in our Thrive Journey, I want you to link arms with the Lord and ensure that He is guiding your every step. I encourage you to commit to a process of prayer that I personally believe will make a critical difference in your entire goal-setting journey.

For the next seven days, I want you to keep a prayer journal. Simply pray each day and ask the Lord to help you articulate a vision for your life, one that will help you focus on the direction He wants you to take. Remember these blessed proverbs:

- "In all thy ways acknowledge him, and he shall direct thy paths" (Proverbs 3:6).

- "Commit thy works unto the LORD, and thy thoughts shall be established" (Proverbs 16:3).

- "A man's heart deviseth his way: but the LORD directeth his steps" (Proverbs 16:9).

We have God's perfect promise that He will support us and guide us, so go ahead, ask Jesus to direct you and write down your prayers each day, along with any thoughts that come to you through prayer or Bible reading. You will find a special place to record all your prayers in your own seven-day prayer journal at the end of this chapter.

Does it make sense to pray for guidance about the future if we are not obeying in the thing that lies before us today? How many momentous events in Scripture depended on one person's seemingly small act of obedience! Rest assured: Do what God tells you to do now, and, depend upon it, you will be shown what to do next.[3] - Elisabeth Elliot.

Prayer Journal

It's time to Thrive!

Simply take a moment to whisper this
prayer to your Savior: I commit the months
ahead to You, my Heavenly Father. I ask
that You help me live each day for Your
glory. I trust in Your precious promise that
You will be my guide, support and friend.

I seek to be all that You want me to be
and do all that You want me to do. Please
guide me through this planning process.
I surrender to do Your will, dear Father.

In Jesus's name I pray,

Amen.

Day One

_____

_____

_____

_____

_____

_____

_____

_____

_____

_____

_____

_____

Day Two

_____

_____

_____

_____

_____

_____

_____

_____

_____

_____

_____

_____

_____

Day Three

_____

_____

_____

_____

_____

_____

_____

_____

_____

_____

_____

_____

_____

Day Four

_____

_____

_____

_____

_____

_____

_____

_____

_____

_____

_____

_____

Day Five

_____

_____

_____

_____

_____

_____

_____

_____

_____

_____

_____

_____

_____

Day Six

_____

_____

_____

_____

_____

_____

_____

_____

_____

_____

_____

_____

_____

Day Seven

CHAPTER 3

It's Time to Dream

> *Ponder the path of thy feet, and*
> *let all thy ways be established*
> *(Proverbs 4:26).*

I will never forget when my eldest daughter started pre-kindergarten. It was our first experience of having a child start school. I was speaking to her teacher one morning when Bethany decided to share her life ambition with all who would listen. She proclaimed with her sweet voice, "When I grow up…I'm going to wear makeup." We broke out into laughter. It was so adorable. She was just three and a half years old. And while we had greater aspirations for her future vocation, this one was most entertaining and memorable.

Let's think for a moment about your dreams and aspirations. Your hopes for the future. I want you to imagine that you're on a winter holiday, sitting in a rustic cabin beside a fire and enjoying your favorite warm beverage. Your friend asks, "Did you have any dreams growing up?" What immediately comes to your mind?

A few of us will quickly be able to share some interesting things we once dreamed of doing, and then there are the typical ones, like perhaps wanting to be a teacher or artist. Then maybe as you grew older, it was all about getting married and having children, owning your own home, or traveling to certain destinations.

Some of us may be able to articulate our life dream, perhaps even some goals. If that's you, then you are one of a small fraction of the population. For the rest of us, it will take intentionality and focus to consider what we truly, deeply desire to accomplish in life (besides surviving another week!).

WHERE TO BEGIN?

Well, if you were reading a secular text, the journey might start with you or perhaps deeper than that; it might start with your heart. It would start with a blank canvas where you could

The journey started when your wonderful Maker thought of you and loved you enough to create you in His image and write an amazing story for your life.

create whatever dream you wanted and empower yourself to achieve it by whatever means you could muster. But as a child of God, the journey started when your wonderful Maker thought of you and loved you enough to create you in His image and write an amazing story for your life. He planned a fulfilling and joyful life for you to live—a life that only a woman with your talents, personality, and spiritual gifts could fulfill.

So the starting point for us as Christian women is different. Our journey started with the One who created us, the One who formed us in our mother's womb and designed us in such a way that we would be perfectly suited to His purpose and for such a time as this. He placed you in a particular era and in a specific family. This time, this way, for His divine purpose.

The Bible teaches that we all have a common purpose and eternal perspective—to glorify our Creator. Yet the way this purpose manifests in our lives is completely unique. Contrary to what most people believe, we need to allow God to write the story of our lives. If we leave Him out of the process, we miss out on the privilege of having His Holy Spirit lead us. Then, as a result, we could miss God's very best for us by attempting to do it alone and in our own strength.

GOD HAS A PLAN FOR YOUR LIFE

> For I know the thoughts that I think toward you, saith the LORD, thoughts of peace, and not of evil, to give you an expected end (Jeremiah 29:11).

God has an *end* in store for your life—a purpose, a destiny, a plan. It's for your ultimate good. His thoughts about you started before you were created. Just read Psalm 139 and marvel at God's amazing care and concern for you personally. He covered you when you were still forming within your mother's womb.

Creation itself reveals the intricate design of its Maker. Consider the solar system, animal kingdom, natural wonders, and the miracle of the human body, living and growing in God's perfect design—people of all cultures and lands are able to see the fingerprints of the eternal God in all creation around them.

You may ask, does God have a specific plan for my life? My

answer is, yes, absolutely. Does He want to reveal His plan to you? Yes, for certain. How? He wants to show you. But how can He show you unless you speak to Him? Never imagine for a moment that you can sidestep a relationship with Jesus and still seek after His plan for your life and succeed. The only way you will achieve God's perfect plan for your life is by abiding in Him, drawing near to Him through prayer and aligning your heartbeat to His. Then and only then will you hear His voice and be filled with the desire to accomplish His will. So now, let's get talking to God.

PRAYER IN ACTION EXERCISE

Grab a timer and set it for five minutes. Use these five minutes to whisper a prayer to the Lord. Ask Him to speak to your heart and to guide your thinking. Dedicate this entire planning process to Him. It may go something like this:

Dear Heavenly Father,

I praise You and thank You for the wonderful God You are and Your work of salvation in my life. I believe You have a special purpose for my life, and I want to trust You to guide my path. Help me now as I set aside this time to seek Your vision. Guide my every thought and step, I pray. I want my life to be pleasing to You. Help me to hold the things of this world loosely and to always be ready to change my plans at Your request.

In Jesus's name,

Amen.

TAKE HEED

Here is a small warning as you progress through your Thrive Journey. Be careful not to bring your own plans before God and simply pray for His stamp of approval. The purpose of a special week of prayer is to listen. There are times when we yearn so badly for something in our lives that we can't even hear what God wants for us—which is always far better than we could possibly imagine. Sometimes we try to open certain doors when God is saying no, perhaps for our protection or out of His mercy. We often find these moments difficult to accept. But when we believe that God desires the best for us, a life laced with His peace and joy, then we will be better able to surrender to His will.

I remember a few times in my career when I applied for a particular job, believing it was precisely the right fit for me; but then the Lord showed me otherwise. Looking back now, I can see how God's hand was in it. He was guiding me each step of the way. I didn't always understand it at the time, but in hindsight I can absolutely see that His path was perfect for me.

When I graduated from university, I applied for graduate positions in various companies. One of the companies I applied at was AMP, a financial services company in Australia. It was a structured graduate role. The successful candidates would spend the first two years rotating in various departments before settling into a fixed role. It sounded like a dream opportunity, with excellent training and prospects. But the Lord did not have a graduate role in mind for me. He had something better planned for me. The Lord allowed for the recruitment manager to see my application and put me forward for a fixed role in the communications department. I couldn't believe it. I had no idea about the role, but because I had worked part-time while studying at university, they were happy to consider my experience and take me on in that position. What did the role involve? Lots of writing. Was it a coincidence? Not at all. As I surrendered to the Lord each step of the way, He beautifully orchestrated the circumstances of my career for my good and His glory.

God's ways are always best, dear sister. His plans are perfect, and His timing is spot on. He is never late and never early. His will is exactly what He created you for and, hand in hand with Jesus, you can be confident that you are on the right path.

> For my thoughts are not your thoughts, neither are your ways my ways, saith the LORD. For as the heavens are higher than the earth, so are my ways higher than your ways, and my thoughts than your thoughts (Isaiah 55:8–9).

OUR FATHER'S HEART

As I began to write this book, my youngest child, Marie-Therese, was 18 months old, and she found climbing up our stairs exhilarating (especially when I was cooking). We added a safety gate at the bottom of the stairs to protect her from making her way up without supervision. Then one afternoon she was desperately desiring to climb up the stairs. She cried and held the bars of the safety gate with expressions of despair. She was so adorable. She scrunched up her little face with disappointment and could think of nothing else than a stair-climbing adventure, which seemed so within reach and yet so far.

I thought of how God must feel when we cry to Him and insist on having something in our life that we're sure will satisfy us. Yet our merciful Father turns to us with great love and at times does not open the door because He sees what is ahead. He knows when danger is lurking. He is all-knowing, so He is in the best position to guide our steps and protect us from future pitfalls. I thought about how I felt two emotions at the same moment—empathy toward my frustrated daughter and confidence that by keeping that gate shut I was keeping her safe. I was willing for her to experience some temporary angst because I knew that was far better than allowing her to have her own way and face a potential disaster (not to mention the importance of accepting that boundaries are in place for our protection and ultimate good).

So, friend, as you travel through this Thrive Journey, please keep an open mind and listen carefully to your Heavenly Father. Be sure to pray with a heart that genuinely desires God's plan for your life. I have no doubt that He will lead you in His perfect path, because this is His eternal, unwavering promise.

In all thy ways acknowledge
him, and he shall direct
thy paths (Proverbs 3:6).

CHAPTER 4

We All Need a Vision

Where there is no vision, the people perish:
but he that keepeth the law, happy is he
(Proverbs 29:18).

An important part of my role as a business consultant is to help organizations clarify their vision. I dig deep into what the company stands for, why they exist, and what they want to achieve. Once they are clear about their vision, we work on their business strategy, priorities, and goals. But it all starts with the vision—then everything they do as an organization begins to flow in that one direction. This is precisely what I would like to help you arrive at in your own life.

The following exercises will help you construct your own personal vision statement, which will help you gain clarity and perspective in your life. Your life vision is the launch pad of your Thrive Plan. It's a simple yet inspiring statement, which captures your life dream.

Colossians 3:1–2 reads:

If ye then be risen with Christ, seek those things which are above, where Christ sitteth on the right hand of God. Set your affection on things above, not on things on the earth.

We have a choice. We can set our affections (mind, passion, heart) on heavenly pursuits, or we can set our affections on earthly pursuits. Clearly the Lord has instructed us to keep our perspective on eternity. That is where our purpose is born and the only realm wherein we can be content. It is the purpose for which we were designed.

As you meditate on this biblical truth, write down in the

following space some words that come to your mind that describe what you believe could be God's vision for your life. You may wish to pray further and ask God to guide you as you jot down some thoughts.

VISIONARY WORDS

_____

_____

_____

_____

_____

_____

_____

It is never too late to start dreaming, setting

new goals and going after them. This is the

very essence of living an intentional life.

LIVING YOUR LEGACY

Before we take the next step to create your life vision statement, let's take a few minutes to think about your influence in this world beyond your life here on earth. Otherwise known as your legacy.

> We have the opportunity to look beyond the here and now and consider what impact we will have on future generations.

Think for a few moments— how do you want to be remembered? What do you want your friends and family to say about you at your funeral (a morbid thought, I know, but a very useful exercise)? As Christian women we have the opportunity to look beyond the here and now and consider what impact we will have on future generations. Meditate on this for a few moments and consider what long-lasting influence you want your life to produce for years to come.

Write your thoughts in the space provided. You can write single descriptive words (like kind, generous, loving, happy) or complete sentences (for example, "She helped me grow in my Christian walk" or "She taught me about true sacrifice"). Simply jot down whatever comes to your mind as you reflect upon the kind of impact you want to have for hundreds of years to come and the memories you want to leave behind.

LEGACY THOUGHTS

_____

_____

_____

_____

_____

_____

_____

_____

Now let's reflect on our legacy thoughts.

1. Inward versus outward focus

Consider how many of the qualities found in your legacy thoughts would be considered *inward* qualities compared to *outward*? For instance, how many relate to your internal *virtues* (for example, character, values, desires, intentions) as opposed to *outward achievements* (for example, your appearance, career, possessions or wealth)? Briefly summarize your insights.

_____

_____

_____

_____

_____

_____

_____

_____

2. Success in the world versus success in God's eyes

Now consider to what extent your legacy thoughts relate to success as the world defines it. Then consider how many relate to success as the Lord defines it in His Word. Summarize your thoughts.

_____

_____

_____

_____

_____

_____

_____

_____

_____

_____

_____

3. Portion of your time on inward versus outward

Finally, how much of your time are you currently investing in building your inward qualities versus your outward achievements? Summarize your thoughts.

_____

_____

_____

_____

_____

_____

_____

Let's never forget the precious words of our Lord as He instructed Samuel in selecting the future king of Israel. He said, "…man looketh on the outward appearance, but the LORD looketh on the heart" (1 Samuel 16:7).

So even when those around you seem overly focused on exteriors, always remember that, ultimately, it's the Lord's opinion that matters. He is interested in the core of our being, the place from which good or bad flows. Of course, when our heart is right with God, more of what we focus on will have an eternal perspective, and what we do with our lives will impact generations to come long after we leave this world.

Allow me to ask you, friend, what difference will your life make for eternity?

I love what Shaunti Feldhahn says in the book *The Life Ready Woman:*

> One of the great benefits of our "era of opportunity" is that once we have that vision and that *way* to make the right decisions on those opportunities, the stage is set for us as women to make an eternal difference in this world![4]

CREATING YOUR OWN VISION STATEMENT

Now, looking at the visionary words you wrote earlier and with consideration to the legacy you want to leave behind, I want you to start stringing together a short, and perhaps inspiring, sentence for your life. Let's call it your *vision statement.* Give it a go in the space provided. I have also offered some examples.

Vision statement examples:

Example 1:

Visionary words: Wife, blessing, generous, kind, gospel focus

Vision statement: To be a kind and generous wife, always taking the time to share the gospel and be a blessing in people's lives.

Example 2:

Visionary words: Helping others, vibrant, mentor

Vision statement: To lead a vibrant life for God's glory. To help and mentor others along the way.

VISION STATEMENT:

_____

_____

_____

_____

_____

If you are struggling to capture your life vision in one sentence, you may create a sentence for each key aspect of your life. For instance, I have a distinct vision statement for my ministry with women, which was particularly important for me as I prepared to write this book.

My women's ministry vision statement:

> I want to empower women to thrive in their Christian walk and make a real difference in their relationships, families, churches, workplaces, communities, country, and the world.

My life vision statement is aligned to my ministry vision; however, it encompasses everything I do.

My life vision statement:

> To glorify the name of Jesus in my life, through the power of His grace, as a godly wife, mother, daughter, sister, and friend. To leave behind a generation who are making a greater difference in this world for God's glory because of Christ living through me.

Two key Scripture verses that fuel my life vision statement are:

- "That the name of our Lord Jesus Christ may be glorified in you, and ye in him, according to the grace of our God and the Lord Jesus Christ" (2 Thessalonians 1:12).

- "To whom God would make known what is the riches of the glory of this mystery among the Gentiles; which is Christ in you, the hope of glory" (Colossians 1:27).

If you have not settled on the perfect sentence or sentences which capture your life vision, please do not despair, because either way you have successfully completed step one of the

Thrive Process. You have started to pray and think about the direction the Lord would have you take in your life, and you have started to draw out the desires or passions currently stirring within your heart.

If you are content to live a reactive life, going with the flow and surviving through life's ups and downs, then stop here. But if you want to thrive in your walk with Christ, then please stay with me. I am confident that the Lord will continue to reveal His vision for your life and direct you as you continue on this journey and seek to make a difference for eternity. Why am I confident? Because it's His promise, and God never goes back on His promises. Remember, "In all thy ways acknowledge him, and he shall direct thy paths" (Proverbs 3:6).

GUIDANCE THROUGH PRAYER

I would like to highlight, once again, the importance of continual prayer. In chapter two I challenged you to pray for seven days for the Lord's direction and to use the prayer journal provided. I would like to encourage you to complete that exercise (if you haven't done so already) and continue the habit in your own life each day. Write down your prayers and any subsequent words or Bible verses that the Lord brings to you during your quiet times. Don't consider this as a chore or duty. Think of it as going for a relaxing spring walk with your Savior—just walking, talking, and receiving His wise counsel. I plead with you, please do not skip this step.

I have found so much joy going back and reflecting on past prayers which I have recorded in my journal. Nothing builds faith more than when you see how God specifically answers your heartfelt prayers over the years.

Prayer is the cornerstone of the Thrive planning process, and without prayer you cannot possibly thrive in your walk with Christ. The moment you stop praying is quite possibly the moment you begin to slowly drift from the heart of what God has planned for your life. And as we know from His holy Word, God makes no mistakes. His ways are perfect, and His instructions for our lives are not grievous. A lack of prayer will hold you back and hinder you from having a clear sense of what you ought to be focusing on right now and into the future. So please, dear sister, open your heart to Jesus and pray.

I will instruct thee and teach thee in the way which thou shalt go: I will guide thee with mine eye (Psalm 32:8).

Part Two

Thrive with a Plan

As we venture into part two of this book, my prayer is that you are enjoying sweet fellowship with your Savior and gaining some perspective about your future. You may have been able to start a prayer journal and benefit from the exercise of consistently praying and writing what God speaks into your life. If writing really isn't your thing, that's okay too; the most important thing is to actually pray. Remember that prayer is one of the most critical aspects of the Thrive planning process. It's through prayer that we join hands with Jesus and invite Him to direct our path.

In the following four chapters you will start to build your own Thrive Plan. That's where your Christ-centered dreams will be narrowed down into specific actions—those that you

will take to help you thrive in your walk with Christ. I pray with all my heart that you will find greater clarity and focus in your life as you follow this Thrive Journey with me.

The Lord bless you.

CHAPTER 5

A Life with Purpose

> *And we know that all things work together*
> *for good to them that love God, to them who*
> *are the called according to his purpose*
> *(Romans 8:28).*

L et's have an open discussion now about the reason you do what you do each week, month, and year. Let me ask you—do you believe that the Lord has given us His precious Word to guide us? If you've chosen to read this book, then I'm assuming your answer is yes. Do you believe that the Bible reveals a number of priorities for your life? I hope you're nodding. Then allow me to ask you this. When was the last time you searched the Scriptures to come up with a list of God's priorities for your life?

Before I start sounding like your Sunday school teacher (forgive me, it runs through my veins), I want to assure you that I intend to keep my promise that this is going to be a simple process. The following exercise had a profound impact on my life, and it would be such an honor for me personally if you would trust me and give it a go.

As I went through this Thrive planning process, I came to realize that there

Intentionality is about living your life with purpose. When you are clear about God's priorities for your life, then you need to be intentional about making them a reality in your day-to-day activities.

were so many opportunities to live out God's purpose in my life right in front of me; I just needed to take the opportunity to pause and get them all down on paper. I truly believe that unless you take a step back and ask God what He wants you to work on and write it down, then you are just going to be guided day by day by everything that's calling for your attention.

Intentionality is about living your life with purpose. When you are clear about God's priorities for your life, then you need to be intentional about making them a reality in your day-to-day activities. The good news is that I'm here to help you achieve this.

YOUR ROLES IN LIFE

Think about who you are now. I promise this is not going to stretch into a deep meditation or mindfulness exercise. I simply want you to think about the roles you have in this life. Or you could call them the hats you wear each day. Perhaps *wife* comes to mind. Or *daughter*. *Mother*, perhaps, or *sister*. *Child of God* or *sister in Christ*. What about *employee* or *employer*? *Ministry worker* or *leader*? *Church member*, *neighbour*, *friend* or *cousin*. *Grandmother* or *aunt*. I could park here all day expanding this list.

As women of God, there are certain roles we all have in common. We are daughters of God. We are sisters in Christ to others at church. We often have some sort of ministry role, not necessarily a formal one but nonetheless a role to play in the body of Christ.

We also have roles that are completely unique to us and utilize our God-given talents, abilities or spiritual gifts. In the following exercise, I want you to consider the roles you play that are unique to the amazing person you are, as well as those you have in common with other women.

Please take five minutes to list all the roles you play in your life. Set the timer and stop at five minutes. Don't be overly consumed with capturing the perfect comprehensive list; in five minutes you will have captured your key roles.

MY ROLES:

_____

_____

_____

_____

_____

_____

_____

_____

_____

_____

_____

_____

Next, I would like you to order the roles you've listed according to their importance in God's eyes—start with a number one next to the most important role from God's perspective and so on. The intention of this task is not to belittle any particular role you have in life, but rather to shed some eternal perspective on this list.

Now I want you to consider the following questions and think about how you are investing in eternally focused responsibilities in your life.

1. Are there roles at the top of your list, in terms of Scriptural importance, which require more of your attention and love? List them here:

_____

_____

_____

_____

2. Are there any roles at the bottom of your list which are taking up the vast majority of your energy, time, and resources? List them here:

_____

_____

_____

_____

Now please take a deep breath. The task of writing down all the roles you hold in life can be overwhelming, I know. Is it any wonder why we so often feel overwhelmed and exhausted? We find ourselves running in many directions, trying to do everything we feel we need to do in order to fulfill these roles, yet lacking peace and fulfillment in the process.

In the following chapter, I will walk you through the next step of the Thrive Journey. I will help you identify what God wants you to focus on, and as a result, you will start experiencing greater clarity and perspective in your life. I can't wait!

If ye then be risen with Christ, seek those things which are above, where Christ sitteth on the right hand of God. Set your affection on things above, not on things on the earth (Colossians 3:1-2).

CHAPTER 6

Your God-given Priorities

> *Trust in the LORD with all thine heart; and lean not unto thine own understanding. In all thy ways acknowledge him, and he shall direct thy paths (Proverbs 3:5–6).*

This step in our Thrive Journey is an eye opener. It's when we get to see that Jesus doesn't want us to have a million focuses at any point in time nor a grand blueprint to be all things to all people. No, the Lord simply wants us to obey

His Word. So the next step in the Thrive planning process is to analyze each of your roles from a biblical perspective. First, you need to consider whether the roles you identified are God-given roles. If you believe that any of the roles you have listed are not of God, take them off your list. These are not the focus of your Thrive Journey.

Next, I want you to select your key roles (roles of most importance) from the first list you made and analyzed in the previous chapter. I'm not going to give you a number, but the roles you select need to be your most significant roles in life, those that require an investment of your time and energy each day in order to fulfill them. Bear in mind that ultimately these roles will play a pivotal part in your Thrive Plan, so you need to be able to list key responsibilities for each of them and prioritize them on a weekly basis. List these most important roles in the space provided.

MY MOST IMPORTANT ROLES:

_____

_____

_____

_____

_____

_____

_____

The roles that don't make it to your list of "most important roles" are not to be ignored. These can be picked up and focused on in the future, but at this stage we are working on a first-things-first basis. It's wise that we seek to gain clarity in our lives by getting intentional about a narrow set of goals (based on our roles of most importance) and work toward achieving them, rather than attempting to produce an endless list of goals that will land us back where we started—overwhelmed and unable to live for Christ with clarity and perspective.

Now it's time for us to start searching the Scriptures. Yes, that's right; you simply need a Bible, pen and the table provided on page 85. Simply write down your top selected God-given roles in the first column, then in the next column start jotting down Bible verses (or just the references) that address God's priorities for you within each God-given role. I know it sounds like a lot of work, but take your time (and yes, you can use an online Bible or Google search). Trust me, this exercise is worth every minute. You will find greater focus if you stick through this process and, as a result, greater freedom to achieve what God wants you to achieve each day.

Next it's time to determine God's priorities for you in each of your God-given roles. Bearing in mind the Scripture you just searched and documented, prayerfully ask the Lord to reveal what His greatest priorities are for you in each of your key life roles. Write them also in the table provided.

This may be completed over a few sittings. Carve out space in your day to do this. It's kind of like decluttering your wardrobe. This is an exercise of decluttering your thoughts, mind, and heart, and finishing the process with clarification and focus from Jesus Himself.

I want you to take your time with this task. The process of fine-tuning your life priorities is not something you want to rush. On the basis of this step, you will be making some important decisions about how to invest your time and what activities to engage in, so please go slowly. Take the time out to soak in God's

Take the time out to soak in God's Word and seek His direction.

Word and seek His direction. The more you invest in this step, the more you'll get out of the entire Thrive Journey. Here is a simple working example to help guide you:

WORKING EXAMPLE

Role	Key Scripture	God-given Priorities
Daughter of God	• 2 Thessalonians 1:12 • Matthew 5:16 • Matthew 28:19 • Proverbs 31: 26	• To glorify Jesus Christ with my whole life • To be different in this world • To share the gospel with others • To speak with wisdom and kindness

Key Role	Key Scripture	God-given Priorities

Table continues over the page.

Key Role	Key Scripture	God-given Priorities

I can personally testify that I walked away energized and excited when I completed this exercise. I found it liberating to be able to capture in one place all the things I had felt a desire to focus on for so long. I was filled with hope and confidence that finally I was going to accomplish more of God's will and purposes for my life.

I love what Terrie Chappell says in her book *The Choice Is Yours*:

When we map our lives by choosing to obey the direction of God's Word, we will not only be spared the harm of our own ways, but we will be happy. We will enjoy the journey! As we learn to apply God's wisdom and the truths from His Word, we will see the reality of Proverbs 3:17–18: "Her ways are ways of pleasantness, and all her paths are peace. She is a tree of life to them that lay hold upon her: and happy is every one that retaineth her."[5]

Wherefore be ye not
unwise, but understanding
what the will of the Lord
is (Ephesians 5:17).

CHAPTER 7

Setting Your Thrive Goals

> *A man's heart deviseth his way: but the LORD directeth his steps (Proverbs 16:9).*

Now it's time to break down your God-given priorities into focus areas. These are areas you need to focus on (sorry to state the obvious), as directed by the Lord through the Scriptures you noted in the previous chapter. For example, perhaps your prayer life has emerged as an area requiring focus in your role as a mother; perhaps sacrifice came up as an area you need to work on in your role of friend. There are no boundaries here. It could seem trivial or mammoth—regardless, when the Holy Spirit brings something to your attention, then it's important. Simply jot these down in the table provided.

Unless you know which areas you need to focus on, more often than not you will completely miss them. You will end up neglecting the aspects of your life that, in fact, require your attention right now.

Key Role	Key Focus Areas

Table continues over the page.

Key Role	Key Focus Areas

Once you have identified focus areas for each of your roles, you need to start thinking about how you could break down those focus areas by identifying SMART (specific, measurable, achievable, relevant and time-oriented) Thrive Goals—goals that are going to help you work toward your overall vision.

WORKING EXAMPLE

Role	Focus Areas
Daughter of God	• Prayer life • Soul winning • Speaking with wisdom and kindness

SMART Thrive Goals

- Create a prayer list and start a new prayer journal this month; incorporate into my daily devotional time with the Lord.

- Pray for opportunities this week to share the gospel with friends or family members who are not Christians. Get acquainted with key salvation verses over the coming weeks.

- Read through Proverbs this month, one chapter each day. Write all the verses that relate to speaking with wisdom and kindness.

SMART Thrive Goals:

Notice that each goal is:

Specific—each goal is clear about what needs to be achieved.

Measurable—it's clear how you can measure success.

Achievable—there's nothing rocket science here; it's all within reach.

Relevant—they are clearly aligned to a particular God-given priority.

Time-oriented—timeframes are clearly specified.

Now it's your turn to work through each of your focus areas and to translate them into SMART Thrive Goals. Again, take your time. This is a pinnacle step in your Thrive Journey.

Key Role	Thrive Goals (SMART)

Key Role	Thrive Goals (SMART)

Congratulations, you now have your **master list** of Thrive Goals.

I love how Elizabeth George lists the value of setting goals in her book *A Woman's Guide to Making Right Choices*. She states the following:

- Goals help define the purpose of your life.
- Goals help develop a set of priorities for your life.
- Goals help determine a focus for your life.
- Goals help drive each day of your life.[6]

I couldn't agree more!

REFINING YOUR THRIVE GOALS

The next step is to pray about the Thrive Goals you have listed. You should have a good set of goals. However, the whole idea is not to feel overwhelmed, so now I want you to prayerfully select one or two goals per role that you want to focus on over the next 12 months. It should be immediately apparent how each of your Thrive Goals will help you work toward fulfilling each particular role. For example: as a mother, select one or two goals; as an employee, one or two goals, and so on. On the following page, write a fresh new list of the goals you will focus on. Keep their description high level. This list is your annual list of Thrive Goals.

ANNUAL LIST OF

Thrive Goals

_____

_____

_____

_____

_____

_____

_____

_____

_____

_____

_____

_____

_____

_____

_____

_____

_____

_____

_____

FINE-TUNING YOUR THRIVE GOALS

Now it's time to refine further. Trust me, it's worth it. Read carefully through each of your Thrive Goals, and work out which of the following categories they fit into. Mark each goal with an A, B or C in your annual list of Thrive Goals according to the following category definitions. As you review your Thrive Goals, you may wish to refine some or merge those that are clearly related.

A. Quick win. It's immediately obvious what you need to do and how you need to go about it. You should also have everything you need in order to achieve these goals. For instance, time, cost, systems, skills, etc. These do not require a significant investment in time or other resources. They are your low-hanging fruit. You can pretty much do these straight-away, so they will be the immediate and first rewards in your Thrive Plan. You will enjoy the feeling of doing what God wants you to do by simply obeying Him and making His priorities your priorities.

B. Further planning required. You are clear about what you want to achieve, but you need to invest more time to plan the goal properly. These are the goals that may appear vague at first glance but hold great reward for those who take the time to flesh them out and translate them into actions. Most people have a desire to achieve these goals, but in the busyness and clutter of life, they don't get the chance to break them down into actions or next steps. So they often end up on the back-burner.

C. New routine, activity or habit. These goals require carving out time in your schedule. You need to add new rituals to your life, whether monthly, weekly, or daily. For example, starting to write in a prayer journal on a daily basis is a new routine. These goals provide wonderful opportunities to disrupt your life and shake out some things that are cluttering your days. When you achieve these kinds of goals, you will feel liberated as you replace unimportant tasks with more eternally-focused tasks.

If you find that all the goals in your master list fall into category A, then skip the following section and go straight to the section titled "Top Three Thrive Goals."

GOALS REQUIRING FURTHER PLANNING

Category B

List your Thrive Goals that fell into category B in the table provided, and then write down the steps you need to take to ensure that you are ready to start working toward these goals. Here is a working example to help guide you:

WORKING EXAMPLE

Category B Goal	Steps for Further Preparation
Sow the seeds of Scripture and salvation in the heart of my children every single day in practical ways.	• Identify the key salvation verses my children need to learn. • Break down the verses and create fun ways for them to learn them.

Category B Goals	Steps for Further Preparation

Category B Goals	Steps for Further Preparation

GOALS REQUIRING A NEW ROUTINE, ACTIVITY OR HABIT

Category C

For goals that require a new routine, activity or habit, it's important that you carve out time in your life to ensure that they actually do become a priority.

Take a moment to consider some activities in your life that you would call time wasters. Some examples may include excessive social media, movies, and unnecessary emails or phone calls.

Think about
your life
as a balance.

On the left sit numerous weights, weighing down your

life. The weights include everything you've considered as a time-wasting activity.

On the right side is where you need time for your new goals. In order to make time for your new goals, you will need to get rid of some of those things on the left which are weighing you down. Make a decision right here and now. What are some activities on the left side of your life that you need to reduce or eliminate in order to create space for your new Thrive Goals? List them in the space provided.

TIME WASTERS

_____

_____

_____

_____

_____

TOP THREE THRIVE GOALS

Okay, so now for the fun part! It's time for you to select three goals (from your annual list of Thrive Goals) that you want to focus on this month. Pray through this. You can't do everything immediately. You need to work through this process; otherwise, you will get overwhelmed with too many things to focus on over a short period of time. Please make sure that each of the three goals addresses a different role in your life. The idea is to impact three separate areas of your life, not to focus specifically on just one role.

Top Three Thrive Goals to focus on this month:

1. _____

2. _____

3. _____

These three goals are what you need to focus on this month. Congratulations! Now, that's focus!

This list now becomes a rolling list of your monthly

Thrive Goals. The idea is that at any given time you will be focused on three Thrive Goals. So at the end of the month, if you have achieved one of your top three Thrive Goals, simply replace it with a new goal from your annual list of Thrive Goals, and so on. If you have a diary, please ensure that your three Thrive Goals are written there and visible to you on a daily basis.

In the next chapter it will become super clear what you need to do to bring your Thrive Goals to life.

It is a safe thing to trust Him to fulfill the desires which He creates. [1] – *Amy Carmichael.*

CHAPTER 8

Achieving Your Goals

> *Redeeming the time, because the days are evil*
> *(Ephesians 5:16).*

Congratulations, you now have an annual list of Thrive Goals and the top three that you will be focused on this month. These goals are no ordinary goals. They are called Thrive Goals because they are grounded in the Word of God and brought to your attention through prayer and searching the Scriptures. How exciting! Now you know what you need to be focusing on.

The next step of your Christ-centered planning journey is to deconstruct your top three goals and map out how you are going to go about achieving them. For each of your top three Thrive Goals, in the spirit of prayer, I want you to think about how you will go about achieving them. Then, in the next table, list two to three steps you need to take for each goal. This may include, for example, making phone calls, arranging a meeting, completing a physical task, prayer, sending emails or messages, creating a mini-action plan, researching a topic, or reading a portion of the Bible or a particular resource. Defining these specific activities is the first step on your journey to achieving your Thrive Goals for this month.

You would have already started this process for goals that fell into category B in the previous chapter. I want you to dig a bit deeper here and get really clear about the next two to three things you need to do next in order to get to where you need to be.

Some of your goals may be straightforward and only require one action. Your larger goals may require more steps.

Regardless, you need to make sure that the next few steps are clear and specific; otherwise, you risk undermining this entire process and could end up with yet another list of perfectly articulated goals that never leave the pretty page you wrote them on.

Also consider eliminating some time wasters in your life to make room for those goals requiring a new routine, activity or habit (category C goals, explained in the previous chapter).

THIS MONTH'S THRIVE GOALS

Top Three Thrive Goals	2–3 Next Steps
1.	
2.	
3.	

A journey of a thousand miles begins

with a single step. – Lao Tzu.

REDEEMING THE TIME

God has blessed us with many helpful resources. One that is of great value and highly perishable is *time*. Time is something you can never get back. Even the richest and most powerful people in the world have no ability to stop or bring back time. The Lord teaches us to use our time wisely.

I want you to open a calendar, whether print or online. I want you to reflect on your typical week. Think about how much time you need to block out for specific tasks. For example, work, the school run, regular unavoidable appointments and so on. After this, look at the optimal times where you are undistracted and able to tackle pretty much anything you want.

Now, start scheduling those steps you have identified above for each of your top three Thrive Goals. I'm talking phone calls, research, reading, writing, meetings— whatever it takes—if you don't schedule it, then you and I know too well that it simply won't happen.

Don't leave your life to chance. Choose to get organized, redeem the time the Lord has entrusted you with, and be super disciplined. At the end of the day, your life will reflect the choices you make. It's your choice how you spend each hour and how these hours make up days and weeks and years of living. What will your choice be?

I love what Elizabeth George says in her book *A Woman After God's Own Heart*:

If you want to know what you'll be like in the future, just look at the choices you are making today...our choices—which reflect our priorities—will determine whether or not we fulfill God's design for our life...whether you are dealing with the next five minutes, the next hour, tomorrow, or forever, the choices you make, make all the difference in the world.[8]

I can truly testify that this Thrive Process works. I have been working toward my own personal Thrive Goals and have experienced the Lord's blessings at each step. This book was one of my Thrive Goals. God placed the burden on my heart to write this book, and when I made it a priority in my life and took steps forward, it became clear that I was going to arrive at my destination. Sure, it was a lot of hard work and required focus and attention, but ultimately the Lord enabled me as I made His will a priority in my life.

BREAKING THROUGH BARRIERS

Let's be honest—life can be very messy. Things come up out of nowhere. Unless we plan ahead for these situations, we will find ourselves overwhelmed and potentially give up on our goals because we just can't deal with hiccups along the way.

The best way to progress through your Thrive Plan and ensure that you achieve your Thrive Goals is to acknowledge up front that hindrances will come. We all have our ups and downs, competing priorities and circumstances. That's life!

And the more prepared we are, the greater the chance we have of continuing our path with resilience.

Let's take some time out now to consider how you will approach hindrances in your life as you work toward your Thrive Goals.

INTERNAL HINDRANCES

Take five minutes now to think about yourself—your emotional state, mindset, attitude, physical body, and spiritual life. Is anything holding you back from achieving your goals? List these in the next table and write at least one action you could take to help conquer each internal hindrance you have identified. I have provided a working example.

WORKING EXAMPLE

INTERNAL HINDRANCE	CONQUER BY
Feeling overwhelmed	• Praying daily, asking the Lord to fill my heart with His peace • Taking the time each afternoon to review my schedule for the next day and reshuffle as needed to ensure that the day is manageable

INTERNAL HINDRANCE	CONQUER BY

EXTERNAL HINDRANCE

Think about circumstances, people or things that are outside your control that may deter you from achieving your goals, and consider how you may approach these. List them in the next table. Again, I have included an example.

WORKING EXAMPLE

EXTERNAL HINDRANCE	MY APPROACH
Accidents, sickness or crisis	• Plan my days with flexibility and stay calm if tasks need to be set aside for a short time • Pray! Remember that God is in control and ask Him what He wants to teach me through the circumstance

Linda Karkafi

EXTERNAL HINDRANCE	MY APPROACH

Well done! Planning ahead for internal and external hindrances will help you navigate your way with greater success.

I love what Amy Carmichael said concerning unexpected things that arise in our lives:

> The best training is to learn to accept everything as it comes, as from Him whom our soul loves. The tests are always unexpected things, not great things that can be written up, but the common little rubs of life, silly little nothings, things you are ashamed of minding one scrap.[9]

So teach us to number our days, that we may apply our hearts unto wisdom (Psalm 90:12).

Part Three

Thrive with Passion

Congratulations, you now have your very own Thrive Plan, which contains your:

- Personal vision statement
- Key roles and life verses
- God-given priorities and focus areas
- Master list of Thrive Goals
- Annual list of Thrive Goals
- Top three Thrive Goals and next steps

What an achievement! My prayer is that you are feeling motivated, energized, and focused toward achieving God's purpose for your life.

Here we are at Part Three, the final part of the Thrive Journey. In the following chapters, you will have the opportunity to ensure that your goals set you up for victory. You will visually capture your Thrive Goals to ensure that

they are kept at the forefront of your mind each day. And you will learn some powerful new daily, weekly, and monthly habits that will enable you to live out your Thrive Goals with intentionality and discipline. I hope you are as excited as I am as we complete this journey together.

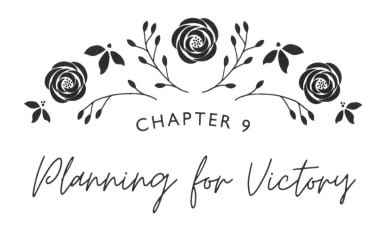

CHAPTER 9

Planning for Victory

> *For with God nothing shall be impossible*
> *(Luke 1:37).*

I t's time to ensure that your Thrive Plan sets you up for victory. Now that you have an annual list of Thrive Goals to work on over the coming year and three goals that you have chosen to focus on this month, it's important to look at some characteristics that need to be evident in your Thrive Plan.

If every plan or set of goals helps us thrive, then why aren't all Christian women thriving? Often we are held back from victory because our goals and plans are lacking certain qualities. So let's explore these together. Notice they make up the acronym T.H.R.I.V.E.

T – TACTICAL

Unless your Thrive Plan contains specific steps that reach to the grassroots level of your life, then it will be no more than a wish list or set of intentions beautifully articulated and ready to be hung up on a wall some place in your home. Unless you dive into your God-given priorities and arrive at some tactical steps to take next, you risk your good intentions remaining just intentions—forever. If your Thrive Plan is not practical in nature, please go back and see where in the Thrive planning process you need to drill down further to arrive at specific goals and steps for further progress. Trust me, it will be worth it.

H – HOLISTIC

Your life, as we learned early in the Thrive Process, is multifaceted. All of us women wear several hats each day and lead busy lives. We have many roles that God has assigned to us to fulfill. It's important that our Thrive Plans reflect this and that our goals extend to all aspects of our lives, rather than being overly focused on one particular role. If you find that your Thrive Plan is skewed toward a particular role or aspect of your life, please go back and ensure that you have followed the steps carefully. Your annual list of goals should have goals that help you thrive across all your God-given roles. If not, simply go back and be sure to select goals that spread across all of your key roles.

R – RETROSPECTIVE

Your Thrive Plan ought to have some retrospective aspects to it. While it is forward-looking, of course, it also ought to consider where you have been and who you are today. It should help move you to be all that God wants you to be now and in the future. Your plan and goals are designed to help you change for the better, grow in Christ, and do more for His glory. They should draw you nearer to Jesus as you seek to live out your God-given roles with passion and intentionality. If you feel that your Thrive Goals are keeping you in the same place, without any stretch or ambition to be better and do more to live out God's purposes for your life— then go back and ask the Lord to help you strive to live more audaciously for His glory. Don't be afraid to take courageous steps forward to make a difference in your life and in the lives of those God has placed around you.

I – INTENTIONAL

The Thrive Plan was born from my desire to live a more intentional life and make a real difference for eternity. The idea of having a Thrive Plan is to thrive in Christ and not just live each day and moment in a reactive and passive manner. So please, think about your Thrive Plan: is it helping you take some important steps forward that are intentional— steps that will help you focus on the things Jesus has brought to your attention through prayer and Scripture meditation? Your Thrive Plan needs to be forward-looking, vibrant, and intentional. It needs to help you redeem the time that God has given you and allow you to take small steps forward toward the big purpose that Jesus has planned for your entire life. If your plan is not intentional in nature, you need to take the time to reframe each of your Thrive Goals and steps so that you are challenged to make decisions that help you live more proactively each day.

V – VIVACIOUS

Does your Thrive Plan energize you and help you approach each day with joy, passion and anticipation? If your plan is a little lackluster and ho-hum, then somewhere along the way you may have stopped dreaming. I encourage you to challenge your thinking and realize that with God you are able to do all things! As Christian women we must never forget how amazing our God is—and since He is able to speak the entire world into existence, then He is able to do so much more in our lives than we have perhaps believed possible. Your Thrive Plan must factor in God's enablement, dear sister. Have a look at your goals and remind yourself that success is possible! Your audacious goals are possible, and with God's enablement you can move forward in areas of your life that you never dreamed you would. Take this leap of faith, trust in your all-powerful Savior, and move forward with confidence. It truly is incredible what the Lord can do through us when we are surrendered to live for Him and ready to live with intentionality each day.

Remember the analogy that Jesus shares in the Gospels about the mustard seed.

In Matthew 17:20 Jesus says, "If ye have faith as a grain of mustard seed, ye shall say unto this mountain, Remove hence to yonder place; and it shall remove; and nothing shall be impossible unto you."

I want to encourage you to believe that with God all things are possible, because that's what He requires us to believe. Be sure that you place your trust in Jesus and not in this process or system. As I mentioned earlier in this book—unless Jesus is at the foundation, in the center, and looped all around our plans, we cannot make a difference for eternity. So be careful what you place your trust in.

I was recently reminded of what it means to have childlike faith by my four-year-old son, Samuel. A few weeks ago, he fell and hurt his foot. At bedtime he asked me to pray that Jesus would heal him. As I knelt beside His bed and finished my prayer, I remembered that I had a jar of ointment I could rub on his foot to reduce any inflammation. I told Samuel about it and then, as I rose up to find it, Samuel said, "No, Mum, I don't want any cream. I want Jesus to heal me." Wow! I immediately thought to myself, *Oh, ye of little faith, Linda.*

E – ETERNAL

Sister, if it's not for Jesus, it's in vain. Please ensure that your Thrive Plan is pointing in heaven's direction. A set of goals that is not Christ-centered and eternally focused will not help you thrive in Christ. I'm not saying they won't help you achieve some good things in your life, but you will lack the joy and contentment that comes when you are in God's will and fulfilling His purposes.

When we are living Christ-centered lives that are sowing seeds for eternity, we can know we are pleasing our Savior. Don't allow your Thrive Plan to be just like any ordinary plan. Allow the Lord to infuse His perspective in your life. Allow Him to direct your path so that you can truly thrive to make a difference with your life.

THE DRIVING FORCE IS FAITH

I hope you have been able to review your Thrive Goals and make any adjustments in light of the six important characteristics your plan should exhibit. Before we move on to the next chapter in this journey, may I remind you of an important driving force for your success and ability to Thrive—faith. Faith in Jesus Christ enables you to accomplish His will in your life.

Six years ago, I made the decision to start my own

company. This was a huge step of faith. I learned that the more I trusted in Jesus and placed my future in His hands, the more I found the courage to face the challenges ahead. You see, I dreamed of being able to work flexibly while my children were at school—to be there for drop offs and pick-ups, to watch them at their carnivals and special events, to study with them, and to make memories together on school holidays—I didn't want to miss a thing. So what happened next? I prayed. I placed my faith in the Lord, and I took a leap of faith. I left my secure and senior role at a leading Australian bank and went out on a limb to fly solo, and the rest is history.

J. Oswald Sanders once wrote:

> Faith enables the believing soul to treat the future as present and the invisible as seen.[10]

In a world that wants to see it to believe it and try it before we buy it, our amazing God gives us faith in what cannot be seen, touched or heard.

Remember today that "Faith is the substance of things hoped for, the evidence of things not seen" (Hebrews 11:1). Without faith we cannot please God, but by faith we can move mountains, sister!

And Jesus looking upon them saith, With men it is impossible, but not with God: for with God all things are possible (Mark 10:27).

CHAPTER 10

Visualize Success

> *And the LORD answered me, and said,*
> *Write the vision, and make it plain upon*
> *tables, that he may run that readeth it*
> *(Habakkuk 2:2).*

Have you ever wondered why you keep forgetting to do certain tasks? Often, it's because you haven't written them down. It's a powerful thing to write down your goals. Many goals are left unaccomplished simply because they are forgotten.

If you desire to live out God's priorities for your life as identified in this whole Thrive Journey, then not only do you need to document your goals (as we have been doing along the way), but even better, you need to find a way to visualize them on a daily basis.

That's why I want to encourage you to create a vision board. Now some of you may be getting excited, thinking of all that lovely stationery and crafty things you can get your hands on. But for those who are already cringing at the thought of a craft project of any sort, please rest assured that I'm not talking about a Pinterest-worthy vision board (but if it happens to be your thing, go for gold!).

The goal here is simplicity. I want you to think of verses, images, quotes, colors, words or anything visual which you can use to represent each of your top three Thrive Goals for this month. Then find a way to visually portray your goals on a board that you can view each day. For example, you want to pray more with your husband, so perhaps show an image of a man and woman praying together. You want to regularly memorize Scripture, then maybe write a few verses that you want to start working on. Whatever you do, simply find a way to capture your top three Thrive Goals on your vision board so that each morning you can see a snapshot of your Thrive Plan for the current month.

Personally, I have found my vision board to be a powerful daily reminder to me of my life commitments. And on those days when I feel disconnected or demotivated, I look at my vision board and remember the end goal. For example, this book would not have been completed if I had not been intentional about writing it. There it was on my vision board in my home office for me to see each day. There were days when I felt I was making no progress at all; however, my vision board helped me remember that this book which God had placed on my heart was going to happen. Because somewhere along the way I received a burden from God to write it, I knew that with His help it would come to pass.

Remember this:

Never doubt in the dark what God has told you in the light. –V. Raymond Edman.

I love this quote! I wrote it in the margin of my Bible. It's such a strong reminder to follow God's direction and leadership, even when things don't make sense and the path ahead seems hard. Isn't that what faith is all about? "Faith is the substance of things hoped for, the evidence of things not seen" (Hebrews 11:1).

We can always have full confidence in the fact that God is in complete control

Remember what He told you in the light, and never doubt that He loves you, is for you, and will never forsake you.

and not one of His promises can fail. His ways are perfect, and His Word is tried. When things feel like they are falling apart, remember the Word of God. Remember what He told you in the light, and never doubt that He loves you, is for you, and will never forsake you.

Your vision board is a way to constantly remind yourself of what God has revealed to you in the light. Allow this step to help you set your affections on things above and to prevent the cares of this world from burying your dreams and the fulfillment of your Christ-centered roles. The women who achieve great things in God's kingdom take intentional steps to ensure they are making progress, and above all, they don't lose sight of God's specific calling on their life. May that be us, sweet sister.

Right now you have three specific Thrive Goals to focus on this month. Visually represent these three goals on a page or board. Then, as you achieve them, take them down and replace them with a new goal from your annual list of Thrive Goals. Watch how amazing you will feel when you know you are taking steps to live out God's plan and purpose for your life. Be sure to also add to your board the visionary words or vision statement that you worked on earlier, in chapter four.

Dream a dream so big that
unless God intervenes it
will fail. - Hudson Taylor.

CHAPTER 11

Thriving as a Way of Life

> *But the path of the just is as the shining light,*
> *that shineth more and more unto the perfect day*
> *(Proverbs 4:18).*

What is the perfect day this verse speaks of? It's the day we enter heaven and all its glory for eternity. It's the day when we no longer are confined by dimensions of time and space. We no longer are under the pressure of deadlines and duty, but rather we enter into true rest in our Savior's arms.

It's the day when we can truly, perfectly thrive in Christ. Until then, we have been given the gift of life here on earth, and we now have the opportunity to live this one life in view of that perfect day.

The path of the just shines more and more, brighter and brighter, as the perfect day approaches. This is our primary purpose here on earth. Throughout this book I have spoken about the importance of thriving. What is the end purpose of thriving? To make a difference here on earth that will have an impact for eternity. Unless your Thrive Goals are centered on that perfect day and perfect life beyond the grave, then it is all in vain.

The path of the just shines more and more, brighter and brighter, as the perfect day approaches. This is our primary purpose here on earth.

So how can we make thriving a way of life? Well, dear sister, I want to encourage you to adopt some good habits to help you start your Thrive Journey and end it well.

Elizabeth George describes a *habit* as being "an action that, due to *repetition*, increases in performance and decreases in resistance. Thus, by *repetition* an action becomes automatic, and a habit—good or bad—is born." Elizabeth goes on to say that "if we stay close beside Him and walk where He guides us, our habits will honor His name, and we'll harvest the fruits of righteousness. We'll develop holy habits!"[11]

So here it goes, friend.

DAILY HABITS

Daily Habit 1

Nourish your spirit: rise up early to pray

> Mark 1:35 says that "in the morning, rising up a great while before day, he [Jesus] went out, and departed into a solitary place, and there prayed."

I want to encourage you, dear sister, to start each day with prayer. Plan to rise before your household, even if it's just 15 minutes earlier. For me, the only way I have been able to consistently achieve this goal in my life is by going to bed earlier on most days of the week. I aim for around seven hours of sleep. Now, I know that with little ones and health situations this is not always possible (a couple of late nights each week tend to be unavoidable), but praying first thing in the morning while nursing a baby totally counts.

Taking the time in the quietness of the morning to pray

and commit your day to Jesus is an excellent habit to establish in your life. It's your opportunity to commit your day to the Lord and ask for His direction, before the demands of life start to invade your thoughts.

I start each day with Jesus because I have come to depend on Him. I know what my days are like when I fail to do this, so I strive to make those days few and far between. I pray that this is, or comes to be, your experience too.

Daily Habit 2

Nourish your mind: consume God's Word

> I will worship toward thy holy temple, and praise thy name for thy lovingkindness and for thy truth: for thou hast magnified thy word above all thy name. In the day when I cried thou answeredst me, and strengthenedst me with strength in my soul (Psalm 138:2–3).

Next I want to emphasize the importance of filling your mind with God's Word each day. This is food for your soul. Even a few verses is better than none at all.

Sometimes we fall into the trap of relying on people or things to give us hope, deliverance and guidance, when the only person who can satisfy us and provide us the perfect guidance is Jesus Christ Himself.

Jeremiah 2:12–13 says:

> Be astonished, O ye heavens, at this, and be
> horribly afraid, be ye very desolate, saith the
> LORD. For my people have committed two evils;
> they have forsaken me the fountain of living
> waters, and hewed them out cisterns, broken
> cisterns, that can hold no water.

Visualize for a moment a large cistern (a tank for storing water), but not merely an ordinary cistern—a broken one! Nearby communities relying on this broken cistern to provide much needed sustenance would be left desolate—because the source they are turning to for their most basic need is faulty. This broken cistern could represent people, places or possessions that we turn to in this world when we should be turning to Jesus. They are enjoyable perhaps for a moment or an hour—but sure enough, the enjoyment abates and no refreshment or satisfaction remains—only guilt, frustration, emptiness, and shame.

But Jesus Himself tells us—I am the fountain of living waters. I provided you with life. I know exactly what you need in order to be fulfilled, equipped, and at rest. Simply come to Me. I will satisfy your thirst. I will not forsake you. I will quench your soul's longing for satisfaction. In Me you can be perfectly content.

So please don't underestimate the importance of this habit in your Thrive Journey. I would go one step further and say that this is the most important habit you could adopt that will directly enable you and empower you to thrive in Christ.

Precious sister, it is through the daily habit of consuming God's Word that we can come to understand who God is and what He wants us to do. At the end of this book, you will find 14 daily devotions for you to enjoy. I hope these will be a blessing to you as you meditate on the precious words of Scripture each and every day.

Daily Habit 3

Nourish your body: eat well and exercise

I don't want to turn this into a healthy lifestyle book, but I do want to encourage you to make healthy choices regarding your body. While I haven't always been consistent in this area of my life (especially during pregnancy and with infants), I can truly say that when I adopt healthy habits, I enjoy greater levels of energy and focus.

For what it's worth, here are my tips that will help you focus on caring for your body the way God intended you to:

- Drink plenty of water.
- Commit to eating more whole foods that will give you the nutrition your body needs to thrive.
- Reduce high sugar snacks and drinks, caffeine, packaged meals and highly processed foods.

- Engage in some form of exercise each day, even if it's just a walk around the block (I know it's tough, but when it's done, it's so worth it, sis).

This is nothing new (there is a plethora of great health advice out there, and I'm in no way an expert), but we need to make choices we know are right. Not start a new diet or follow some health fad; no, just simply making some positive adjustments and following them with commitment. Each time you are tempted to neglect your body and vitality—remind yourself how great it feels to be nourished and healthy on the inside.

Sister, if you want to thrive in your life, you don't want to be held back by a body that's lacking energy and nourishment. Give your body what it needs to thrive, and you will feel so much better for it.

WEEKLY HABIT

Plan your week ahead

Invest ten minutes each weekend to pray and plan for the week ahead. Review your Thrive Goals and make sure the key steps you need to take in order to achieve them are scheduled in, along with the other important activities in your life like exercise routines, meal planning, kids' activities, work commitments, special occasions, and so on. Knowing what needs to get done in the week ahead will enable you to make wise choices about your time and will bring you closer to achieving your Thrive Goals.

MONTHLY HABITS

At the end of each month, reflect on the month that has just passed and consider the following habits:

Monthly Habit 1 – Reflect on your progress

Taking time to recognize how far you have come is so important. Today's culture seems to be all about the hustle; however, in Scripture we learn the importance of rest and reflection. Take some time out to reflect on God's work in your life over the previous month.

Ask yourself—what can I do better, differently or more of next month in order to improve the way I am living out my Thrive Goals? Make sure you write down your key learnings in a diary or journal. This kind of specific reflection will help you become more effective with every passing month and ensure that you are continually improving.

Acknowledge your successes and be sure to praise the Lord for His guidance. Share your progress with your family and friends, and celebrate your milestones. Be sure to give God the glory.

Monthly Habit 2 – Review your Thrive Goals

Have a look at your top three Thrive Goals. Do you need more time to continue working toward them? That's not a problem. Simply make them your top three goals again next month. Each time you achieve one of your top three goals, simply replace it with a new goal from your annual list of goals. If you feel you have scope to add an extra Thrive Goal to this month's list, then go for it. But remember, each time you select a new goal to focus on, be sure to list the next 2-3 steps you need to take in order to start working toward the goal.

While the Thrive planning process gives structure to planning your life goals, it also allows you to be flexible. Life is ever-changing. You may have more scope in a particular month to work on your Thrive Goals than a subsequent month. And that's okay. Take the opportunity to adjust your schedule each month. As long as your Thrive Goals are a priority, then you are on track to living a more intentional life.

Monthly Habit 3 – Refresh your Thrive vision board

Your Thrive vision board was never designed to be a set-and-forget project. Each month I want you to refresh your vision board. This doesn't need to take more than five minutes. Simply make sure that your top three Thrive Goals for the month ahead are clearly represented.

Reviewing your vision board and making sure it reflects what you want to focus on each month is important. Make sure it's in a place where you can view it each day, preferably early in the day. The more often you look at your vision board, the more often you will find yourself recalling it throughout the day in the moments when you need it most.

YEARLY HABIT

Revisit your Thrive Plan

I recommend that either toward the end of each year (you may want to do this before the Christmas rush) or at the beginning of the year, you revisit your Thrive Plan and make adjustments, additions or updates as required. A lot happens in a year, and you want to make sure that your Thrive Goals are still relevant.

Take some time to pray about your vision and add new dimensions that God has revealed to you in more recent months. Briefly look over part two of this book, along with your responses to the exercises. Be sure to check out the roles you listed at the beginning of your Thrive Journey and particularly those roles that may not have been at the top of your list over the past 12 months. They may require greater focus in the year ahead.

BE FLEXIBLE, BUT REMAIN CONSISTENT

I know that life does not always allow for a methodical approach to planning your life. I get that. And that's not what the Thrive journey is meant to be. Now that you have experienced the first round of the Thrive process in your life, you will find the review stage a piece of cake. Once you get the concept, process, and end result, you will be able to adjust the steps to serve you better (particularly during tumultuous seasons in your life). You can allow some stretch in your plans and give yourself more time to work on each goal as needed. At the end of the day, as long as you are committed to living out your God-given vision, priorities, and goals, then sister, I believe you are thriving.

This one simple act of beginning each day with God sets each day on the path of wisdom. [12] - Elizabeth George.

It's Time to Thrive

*That ye might walk worthy of the Lord unto
all pleasing, being fruitful in every good work,
and increasing in the knowledge of God
(Colossians 1:10).*

Congratulations on successfully completing your Thrive Plan. I am so excited about your journey ahead as you seek to thrive in your life with Christ and make a real difference for eternity. I truly believe that together we can make an impact on this world as we intentionally seek to live out our God-given roles and priorities. The disciples turned the world upside down, and I believe with all my heart that as Christian women, we can change the world one intentional step at a time.

Imagine a world where all women are living out their intended purpose—godly, surrendered and Christlike. This side of heaven, we can't imagine a world where all women are living so triumphantly. However, we can imagine a life for ourselves where we are no longer allowing the world to dictate our decisions, but rather allowing Jesus to set our life priorities and then surrendering to live them out with passion and commitment.

Revolutionizing your life with Christ is a step-by-step process. If you truly want your life to count for Christ, I encourage you to keep praying and inviting Jesus to help you live a triumphant and victorious life for His glory. The Lord did not create you to live a defeated and discouraged life. He wants more for you. He wants you to absorb His Word and live it out for all to see that He is Lord! Sister, let today be the start of a new chapter in your life. May you, like never before, surrender to live your life in a way that makes a difference for eternity.

So, sister, are you ready to thrive?

Allow me to remind you that God has the perfect plan for your life. The perfect set of priorities for you to focus on. The perfect way to go about achieving His milestones for your life. And the perfect ending.

Does that mean we will have perfect days and perfect families, with the perfect white picket fence we've always dreamed about (okay, so maybe that's my dream)? The answer is no. Rather, thriving is about living each day knowing that in the stillness of prayer and through the study of Scripture, you got a glimpse into God's purpose for your one precious life. You acknowledged that you have been blessed with the time, talents and resources from God to live out that purpose, and you made a decision to walk in that direction.

As a result, you have the opportunity to live in a way that

honors God, glorifies Him and is far better than a life of stumbling along, struggling along, striving along—hoping that somewhere, somehow you have accomplished something God wants you to do. You'll be a better mother, a better wife, a better sister, a better friend, a better woman—because you have chosen not to settle for a life without focus. Instead, you've been

> You'll be a better mother, a better wife, a better sister, a better friend, a better woman—because you have chosen not to settle for a life without focus.

careful with the resources God has given you and have done your best to direct them toward His intentions for your life and His focus on eternity.

Do I thrive every day? No, my friend. Some days I still feel like I'm reacting all day and putting out fires. But I can truly say that in moments of despair, confusion and frustration, I have a plan. I have something to go to which is Christ-centered and biblically rooted—it reminds me of who I am. It gives me Bible verses to help me keep my eyes on Jesus and to discern what is the next right thing I need to do. And let's be honest, sometimes the next right step is all we need to know and all we can handle.

Thrive planning is not the next new big thing every woman needs. It's just a simple, helpful, biblically grounded system to help you apply God's Word to your own individual life. It's designed to help you remain focused on what God wants you to do and how He wants you to go about achieving it. Thrive planning is about setting your priorities straight with your Savior. Perfection will come in heaven. Until then, life is about living each week, day, and moment to our fullest, to the glory of God the Father.

My prayer is that you will allow your Thrive Plan to infuse passion into your life. And if you remember nothing else I have written, please remember this—you have just one shot at life, one chance to be a wife, mother, soul winner, daughter, sister, friend, and mentor. You have just one chance to live out God's priorities for your life.

May the Lord help you to make your one life count enormously for God's glory and for the sake of His glorious gospel.

God bless you, precious sister, and let's thrive together to make a difference for eternity!

The LORD bless thee, and keep thee: The LORD make his face shine upon thee, and be gracious unto thee: The LORD lift up his countenance upon thee, and give thee peace (Numbers 6:24-26).

Daily Devotions

Day 1: Seek Him First

> *But rather seek ye the kingdom of God; and all these things shall be added unto you (Luke 12:31).*

I would like to encourage you with a thought that the Lord impressed upon my heart last week. With several priorities and things to do, I found myself being pulled in many directions. Some moments I felt overwhelmed and flustered. Through this portion of Scripture, the Lord reminded me how I can be sure that my priorities are right and that my needs will be met.

The Lord knows precisely what I need. He knows what my family needs. He knows what my children need. When faced with so much to do and so much to think about, it's wonderful when the Lord says, just pause for a moment—just focus on this one thing that's needful, just seek My kingdom first. Set your heart on things above. Just look up! And all these things—activities, to-do's, priorities, needs, and goals— all of it will fall into place because you have trusted in Me.

The words that stood out to me in an earlier verse (verse 29) were "neither be ye of doubtful mind." Wow! How often when we feel overwhelmed with our life priorities do we start to doubt? Can it all be done? Can it be done well? Can I get through this week? Can I succeed in this pursuit? Yet, Jesus says, "Do not doubt in your mind. Just believe."

Whatever you have on your plate today, may I encourage you to lift up your eyes and seek Jesus. Ask for the courage and strength to do all things well—those things that are important to Him.

Remember these precious truths. All the other things will be added unto you. He knows your needs perfectly and promises to provide for you. Don't doubt; replace your doubt with faith, for with God all things are possible!

May the Lord bless you and give you wisdom to live out each of your priorities well today and for His glory.

Daily Devotions

Day 2: Never Compromise

> *If it be so, our God whom we serve is able to deliver us from the burning fiery furnace, and he will deliver us out of thine hand, O king. But if not, be it known unto thee, O king, that we will not serve thy gods, nor worship the golden image which thou hast set up (Daniel 3:17-18).*

Three faithful men faced the fire of persecution: Shadrach, Meshach, and Abednego. They chose to give their worship and praise to God alone.

The idol of their day was a golden image. It was convenient to join the crowd. It would support their position in society. Their response was simple: "…we will not serve thy gods, nor worship the golden image which thou hast set up" (Daniel 3:18).

Three simple words: *we will not.* What is vying for your attention today? What's seeking a place in your heart? What issue is challenging your faith? I encourage you to choose these three simple words: *I will not.* I will not compromise. I will not conform. I will not consider. I will not concur. Whether idol or ideology, preference or practice, lifestyle or logic, may we choose to stand firm on the Word of God, despite the pressure, and commit to saying, "I will not."

Notice that God did not stop them from entering the fiery furnace. But He chose to stand with them. They were safer in that fire than anywhere else in the region, for they were with God Himself. And the fire did not consume them.

Sisters, I don't know what fire of persecution or pressure you are facing today. But I know one thing for certain: your Heavenly Father is right beside you. Say, "I will not" to the evil and "I will" to the pure. Jesus will walk with you through the fire, and you will not be consumed.

> When thou passest through the waters, I will be with thee; and through the rivers, they shall not overflow thee: when thou walkest through the fire, thou shalt not be burned; neither shall the flame kindle upon thee (Isaiah 43:2).

Choose to live on higher ground and trust that your Savior will be right there beside you no matter what.

Daily Devotions

Day 3: What's in Your Hands?

> *Whatsoever thy hand findeth to do, do*
> *it with thy might; for there is no work,*
> *nor device, nor knowledge, nor wisdom,*
> *in the grave, whither thou goest*
> *(Ecclesiastes 9:10).*

A rod in the hands of Moses. A hammer in the hands of Noah. A sling in the hands of David. What did these great men of the Bible have in common? They were ordinary men living ordinary lives, but they each served an extraordinary God who could do wonders with their little faith and whatever was in their hands.

When God called Moses to release His people from bondage in Egypt, Moses said to God, "But, behold, they will not believe me, nor hearken unto my voice" (Exodus 4:1). To which the Lord replied, "What is that in thine hand?" (Exodus 4:2).

Often the Lord will ask us to do something, and our first reaction is, But...? But how will it work? But what if I fail? But what will people think? Sister, the Lord doesn't want you to figure it all out. He simply wants you to trust Him and obey. What's in your hands today, precious sister? May I remind you that God can do wonders with whatever He places in your hands. Your singleness, marriage, motherhood, home, work, business, education, talents, health, and the list goes on.

He can do miracles through you if you simply surrender to Him. You may be thinking, *But I'm just surviving each day and week.* Trust Him. The God of Moses is your God too. He had just come through some heavy personal circumstances— killing an Egyptian, running away from Pharaoh's palace where he was raised, and now living as a shepherd in Midian. The last thing he thought he'd see that day was God in a burning bush! He had no idea what was in store for his life. He certainly didn't think we would be reading about him today in admiration and using his life as an example of faith and obedience. But he took the next step. He cast that rod on the ground before God and believed that He was able to do something special with his life. And wonders followed, my friend.

May the Lord do wonders through your precious life, sister, and use whatever is in your hands for His glory. Take a moment to meditate on this question—is there something in my hands today that I can surrender to the Lord?

Daily Devotions

Day 4: Here Am I, Lord; Send Me.

> *Also I heard the voice of the Lord, saying,*
> *Whom shall I send, and who will go for*
> *us? Then said I, Here am I; send me*
> *(Isaiah 6:8).*

Over the years there have been times when I have been particularly touched by a sermon or been at a crossroad in my life, and my response was a prayer of surrender. But I wonder, could we be missing out on amazing opportunities to serve the Lord and experience His power in our lives because we don't daily surrender to Him?

Isaiah 6:8 is not an exclusive verse to missionaries. The world is in dire need of hope. People are desperate for truth. Our families, colleagues and friends are desperately in need of Jesus, and what is our response? What part are we playing? What hope are we giving?

I'm concerned that our lives (mine first) can get so busy that we no longer ask Jesus to send us, to use us or to speak through us. Our prayers are more often about making our lives more comfortable. Perhaps we need to ask Jesus to make us more uncomfortable so that we feel the grief of people around us and become channels of grace in the lives of others. Let us never forget that we have hope. We have the answers. We have received His promises. Now more than ever we need to pass on the love.

Wherever this devotion finds you today—at your breakfast table, on the way to work, caring for your child, cleaning your home, at the office—whatever you are doing, simply stop for a moment and whisper a prayer to your Savior: "Here am I, Lord, send me."

Tell Him you are available, and you will see how God will bless your surrendered life and use you in ways beyond imagination. From my experience, there is no greater joy than being used by God to be a blessing in the life of another human being. No career, no material possession, no friendship nor success comes close to the joy you receive from seeing the God of this universe use you.

Daily Devotions

Day 5: God's Word Stands

> *The grass withereth, the flower fadeth: but*
> *the word of our God shall stand for ever*
> *(Isaiah 40:8).*

Life as we know it has changed. How many times have you heard this statement or a variation of it? The COVID-19 global pandemic shook our foundations and stripped us of freedoms we thought we could never lose.

Freedom to gather. Freedom to embrace. Freedom to celebrate. Freedom to worship. Freedom to come and go as we please. Who would have thought that news of case numbers, border closures, vaccinations, and quarantine would become our daily media digest?

But you know what, we serve the living God who knew about the pandemic before it occurred. Before the first media outlet reported that in China a fatal virus was spreading and destroying thousands of lives, He knew. And there was something He gave us before it all changed our lives, something that would never change. Something that would stand the test of time and all possible viruses or variations of viruses. And that's His perfect, infallible, holy Word. It stands forever!

I thank God that while the things of earth come and go, I have the Word of God to affix my heartstrings to. I choose to build my life on something steadfast, true, and eternal—the precious Word of God.

When you feel your foundation is a bit shaky, remember the Word of God. It stands forever. It stands the test of time, and it will get you through.

May the Lord strengthen your heart and your resolve to build your life on the Lord Jesus Christ, for His Word will never change and He will never let you down.

Daily Devotions

Day 6: Place Your Trust in Jesus

> *Why do we find it difficult to be in complete*
> *confidence in God? Because it is hard to*
> *trust someone that you do not know.*
> *– Adrian Rogers.*

Ouch! How very true. The more we know the Lord—like, really know and experience His goodness, promises and faithfulness—the more we should place our trust in Him and rest in His will for our lives.

In a culture that revolves around instant gratification, we can learn to have faith in the unseen things of God. The Bible teaches us that "Faith is the substance of things hoped for, the evidence of things not seen" (Hebrews 11:1). By faith we can hope for better things and see God work in amazing ways.

God grants us faith and grows our faith, but He desires for us to exercise our faith in the steps we take each day.

This morning I read about the woman with a sickness that had plagued her for 12 long years. She was desperate for healing and recovery. No doctor or physician could provide any answers. She was at the end of all hope. So she went to Jesus. She desired to touch Him, to reach out and experience His power in her life. And she received it. Her confidence was unwavering. She believed that just one moment, just one touch, would bring her healing, to which Jesus proclaimed, "Daughter, be of good comfort; thy faith hath made thee whole" (Matthew 9:22).

Whatever your struggle, pain or difficulty is today—may I encourage you to take it to Jesus. You can have complete confidence that He will help you, draw near to you, and give you exactly what you need.

Remember that God is on your side. The Creator of all things, the Redeemer and Sustainer of life—He is going before you. He will guide you. He will protect you. He will never leave you. Nothing catches Him by surprise. He loves you and is orchestrating your life for your good and His glory.

Daily Devotions

Day 7: God Is Good in the Wilderness

> So Moses brought Israel from the Red sea,
> and they went out into the wilderness
> of Shur; and they went three days in
> the wilderness, and found no water
> (Exodus 15:22).

The children of Israel are triumphantly rescued from slavery; they are singing and glorifying the Lord for their great escape. Then they hit dearth. It's hot. It's dry. And they're reminded of their most basic need—water. They travel for three days, but there's no water. Finally, they arrive at the waters of Marah, but it's a bitter discovery. Exactly what they need is right before them, but it won't quench their thirst. It's bitter. The people are frustrated. They murmur with desperation. The Lord was preparing full deliverance; they just needed to pass through the wilderness first. God had work to do in their hearts before they could be ready to handle the battles ahead. So the Lord intervenes. He keeps His promises.

What did Moses do next? The perfect thing to do when faced with an insurmountable challenge—he cried unto the Lord! The Lord provides the perfect remedy: a tree. A beautiful symbol of the cross of Calvary. Moses obeys God's instructions. He casts the tree into the waters, and… "the waters were made sweet" (Exodus 15:25).

Sister, I don't know what path you are travelling on right now, but perhaps you have found yourself looking out at some bitter circumstances in your life and you're not sure what to do next. May I suggest that you take these simple steps:

1. Take it to the cross.
2. Trust in God's promises.
3. Obey His Word.
4. Wait on Jesus to sweeten your bitter waters.

Remember, deliverance is coming!

Last night as I was putting my girls to bed, my eldest daughter was sweetly reading this verse out loud: "But whosoever drinketh of the water that I shall give him shall never thirst; but the water that I shall give him shall be in him a well of water springing up into everlasting life" (John 4:14). How suitable.

Precious sister, never forget: Jesus loves you, Jesus has the remedy, and Jesus will sweeten your bitter circumstances. Just trust Him, and He will see you through.

Daily Devotions

Day 8: The Depths of Christ's Love

> *For he shall grow up before him as a tender plant, and as a root out of a dry ground: he hath no form nor comeliness; and when we shall see him, there is no beauty that we should desire him (Isaiah 53:2).*

It's a solemn read but a rich prophetic description of the humble, earthly beginnings of the Messiah—Jesus Christ, the Son of God. It sets the scene for the glorious gospel of Christ.

It's difficult to fathom that the King of Kings would put aside His glory to be born into this wretched, messed-up world to save sinners like you and me. He chose a family without reputation or social status. Born to a poor carpenter. The root out of a dry ground. It was thought that no good thing could come out of the region He was born into. With neither exceptional beauty nor status to recommend Him, He walked in our shoes as One who was reduced and ready to bear our grief and sorrows.

Please consider for a few moments the great lengths that Jesus went to in order to prove to you that He loves you. Consider how He was willing to forsake all His rights and glory to reach your soul.

While Isaiah 53 often fills our hearts with somber thoughts of the sufferings of Christ, when we meditate on them, we see the shades and depths of love our wonderful Creator had for us and can truly rejoice!

Rejoice with me today, dear sister, with all your heart, for truly you and I are greatly loved. We are loved not in word alone, but in the sacrifices of our Savior which run deep and wide throughout history.

May your heart experience the unconditional, limitless and indescribable love of Christ, now and always.

For I am persuaded, that neither death, nor life, nor angels, nor principalities, nor powers, nor things present, nor things to come, Nor height, nor depth, nor any other creature, shall be able to separate us from the love of God, which is in Christ Jesus our Lord (Romans 8:38-39).

But God commendeth his love toward us, in that, while we were yet sinners, Christ died for us (Romans 5:8).

Greater love hath no man than this, that a man lay down his life for his friends (John 15:13).

Daily Devotions

Day 9: Jesus Felt Your Pain

> *Surely he hath borne our griefs, and carried our sorrows: yet we did esteem him stricken, smitten of God, and afflicted (Isaiah 53:4).*

When we feel like no one understands what we're going through, we can find respite in Jesus. As we reflect on this awesome truth today, may I remind you that Jesus is acquainted with your grief. In fact, not only is He acquainted or familiar with your grief, but He bore your grief! And if that wasn't enough, He also carried your sorrow.

In the middle of the night, this thought came to me—*how did Jesus bear our grief and carry our sorrows? Then I thought— what is the cause of our sadness and misfortunes in life? What is the cause of our illnesses, hurts, sorrow, and despair? Is it not sin?* The root cause is always sin. Sin entered this world and caused the fall in the garden of Eden, and as a result, death and sin spread across all humanity. Sickness, pain, and broken fellowship are all far-reaching effects of sin.

Then, there is our own sin and rebellion. Sadly, our sins cause us to stumble and mess up our lives, bringing about more grief. And finally, there are the sins of others and the consequences they bring about in our lives—causing hurt, anxiety, and distress in us and our loved ones. Sin is always the problem.

So then, how does our blessed Savior bear our grief and carry our sorrows? He became sin for us. He who knew no sin took upon Himself the sting, judgment, and condemnation of sin, and nailed it to His blessed body on the cross.

Jesus dealt with the root cause of all our problems—sin! And so today, may we rejoice yet again, for we do not have a high priest "which cannot be touched with the feeling of our infirmities" (Hebrews 4:15).

He understands you, sister. He knows exactly what you're passing through. Take all your grief and sorrow to the cross and enjoy the perfect empathy, grace, and peace that only He is in a position to give.

Daily Devotions

Day 10: Live in Light of the Cross

> *But he was wounded for our transgressions,*
> *he was bruised for our iniquities: the*
> *chastisement of our peace was upon him;*
> *and with his stripes we are healed*
> *(Isaiah 53:5).*

What spurred the Savior to suffer such agony—physically, emotionally, and spiritually? It was you, dear friend. His love for you was so deep and so wide that He willingly laid down His life, position, and dignity to provide you with protection from hell, purpose in this life, and peace beyond comprehension.

Are you living the good Christian life? I'm not asking if you are a good Christian. I'm asking if you are living the good life for which Jesus hung upon the cross? Are you enjoying the forgiveness of your sins? Are you at peace with the fact that you are loved and cared for by your Maker? Are you enjoying opportunities to serve God and live in fellowship with Him and other believers?

Beloved sister, the abundant Christian life was purchased with the blood of Jesus Christ on Calvary. This is why Jesus suffered, for our benefit and for our good. And so, what's next? Shall we accept mediocrity or be spurred to rise up further and serve Jesus with greater rigor, passion, and love because we so appreciate what He sacrificed for us? I pray that it may be the latter. May we be fueled with passion to serve Him more and grow in His grace because we love Him and appreciate all that He has done for us.

I love what Matthew Henry said:

Christ was in pain that we might be at ease, knowing that through him our sins are forgiven us. Hereby we have healing; for by his stripes we are healed. [13]

Sister, what will you do differently today in light of the cross? We have the opportunity to thrive in Christ today because of what Jesus did that day at Calvary. May we not waste another moment living for this life, but rather for eternity.

Daily Devotions

Day 11: Trust in the Lord

> *What time I am afraid, I will trust in thee*
> *(Psalm 56:3).*

It's time that we replace our fear with faith. Fear takes many forms. Anxiety, worry, doubt, apprehension, deep concern— they engrave themselves a home deep in our minds and hearts. But when their false voices arise in our lives, how do we silence them?

David made a strong resolution: "I will trust." In Psalm 56:3 David suggests that the best response to fear is placing your trust in the Lord. And David was fearful of death. Yet he knew that God alone could be trusted.

What's causing you to fear today?

- Are you afraid for your children, spouse or parents?

- Are you afraid about work, finances or your lifestyle?

- Are you afraid of the challenges you face today, and tomorrow, and the day after that, and the day after that?

Sister, we all fear. We all worry. We all dread. But what makes us victorious as daughters of Christ is in Whom we place our trust during those moments of fear.

May we trust in Jesus and not our circumstances. May we trust in His provision and not our wealth. May we trust in His kindness and not in how our friends can support us. And may we trust in His deliverance and not in this world's false promises.

God is so good. He has the answers. He loves you beyond measure, and He will deliver you. Simply trust Him even when you don't feel like it. Just trust Him. Then walk by faith, and He will deliver you from all doubt and fear. Say it out loud, sister. *What time I am afraid, I will trust in thee.*

Daily Devotions

Day 12: In Christ Alone

> *My soul, wait thou only upon God;*
> *for my expectation is from him*
> *(Psalm 62:5).*

We don't always intend to, but we often do place our expectations in people, prospects or possessions. Then when they fall short of what we hoped for, we feel disappointed.

I am reminded in this simple yet powerful verse that our expectations ought always to be set on Jesus. As we wait on God, hope in Him, and trust Him, we need to align our hearts to Jesus in such a way that we are expecting only Him to provide.

He promises us time and again that He will be our provider

and the source of all hope, strength, love, joy, peace, and the list goes on. Yet we quickly forget and turn to the promises this world makes about the very things Jesus has promised to give us—freely and in abundance!

What are you turning to in order to fulfill your heart's desires? Your marriage, children, friends, properties, cars, holidays, career or personal fitness? It's not always so obvious; we often place our trust in these things without realizing it. We all do it. But today, let us take the opportunity to meditate on this question: What am I expecting from people, possessions or prospects that only Jesus can fulfill?

Then pray:

Please help me, Lord, to place my hope in You alone and for all my expectations to be set on You. Thank You for Your promises to provide all my needs. Help me to trust You and for my soul to be content with all that You provide each day.

In Jesus's name I pray, Amen.

God bless you, precious sister, and may we together remember that when our expectations are set in Christ alone, we will never be disappointed. For He is good and faithful and ever so kind.

Day 13: Choosing to Forgive

> *And be ye kind one to another, tenderhearted, forgiving one another, even as God for Christ's sake hath forgiven you (Ephesians 4:32).*

When Joseph was faced with his painful past, he had a choice: to fight or forgive. He chose to forgive. He could see God's divine hand in his misfortunes. I can never get over his response. What a powerful example of forgiveness and restoration:

And Joseph said unto them, Fear not: for am I in the place of God? But as for you, ye thought evil against me; but God meant it unto good, to bring to pass, as it is this day, to save much people alive.

Now therefore fear ye not: I will nourish you, and your little ones. And he comforted them, and spake kindly unto them (Genesis 50:19–21).

There were no coincidences in Joseph's tumultuous life journey. It was filled with much hurt. There were painful memories of rejection and isolation. But at the end of the journey, God gave him insight into the pain. He came to understand there was a purpose in it all, and in that purpose, Joseph found healing.

Joseph was able to forgive his brothers because he believed in the One who held him through it all. It didn't prevent the painful memories from creeping up and bringing him momentary sorrow every now and then. When his brothers spoke to him, asking him for forgiveness after his father died, we see Joseph weeping. He had experienced triumphant success in his life; even so, the pain of his past did hurt when it reared its ugly face again. But he found comfort in the Lord.

And who doesn't love a happy ending? At the end of Genesis, we read how Joseph is enjoying his great grandchildren upon his knees, the children of Machir the son of Manasseh. And how lovely to recall the meaning of Manasseh—"For God, said he, hath made me forget all my toil, and all my father's house" (Genesis 41:51). Isn't it wonderful when our Savior works all things together in our lives for good? He allows us to move forward and forget our toil and pain, as we fix our heartstrings on Jesus.

May the Lord help you, dear sister, to forgive past hurts and fill you with His perfect comfort and peace.

Daily Devotions

Day 14: If It Brings You Closer to Jesus, It's Worth It

> *And not only so, but we glory in tribulations also: knowing that tribulation worketh patience; And patience, experience; and experience, hope: And hope maketh not ashamed; because the love of God is shed abroad in our hearts by the Holy Ghost which is given unto us (Romans 5:3-5).*

Dear friend, this is for you today. It's for you and every other human being on this earth who carries burdens. Whether it's a challenging circumstance, a difficult relationship, parenting woes, health issues, or you fill in the blank. I want to remind you to take your burdens to Jesus. Pray about every single part of your concerns, fears, and frustrations. Take it to the cross and leave it there by faith.

Don't despise your circumstances, but rather embrace them as vehicles of change in your life. Allow Jesus to use them in your life for good (Romans 8:28)—to make you stronger, teach you lessons, increase your faith, open new doors or prepare you for future events.

As a child of God, nothing enters your life without God's permission, so embrace the hard moments, trusting with all your heart that Jesus loves you, that He has a purpose in it— for your good and His glory.

In 2 Corinthians 4:17-18, the Bible says:

> For our light affliction, which is but for a moment, worketh for us a far more exceeding and eternal weight of glory; while we look not at the things which are seen, but at the things which are not seen: for the things which are seen are temporal; but the things which are not seen are eternal.

What a wonderful reminder to us of the importance

of having an eternal perspective. In light of eternity, our afflictions are momentary. While our trials often feel like they are permanent, God reminds us that they are temporary.

I pray that the Lord fills you with faith, resilience, hope and comfort through all the trials that come your way. And remember, dear friend, just as the sun will always rise in the morning, you can be sure that the love and grace of God is steadfast, sufficient, and available to you every moment of every day.

Never forget—if it brings you closer to Jesus, then it's worth it.

The Gift of Eternal Life

The Bible clearly states that we are all sinners. We have all fallen short of God's perfect standard. Romans 3:23 says, "For all have sinned, and come short of the glory of God." Also Isaiah 53:6 reads, "All we like sheep have gone astray; we have turned every one to his own way; and the LORD hath laid on him the iniquity of us all." The problem is that our rebellious sin must be punished. Just like a judge hands us a verdict when we break the law, God, who is perfect and fair, must punish us for our sin.

The first part of Romans 6:23 says, "For the wages of sin is death." This means that sin in our lives leads to death. Not just physical death, but also spiritual death. Because God is holy and perfect, He cannot bear to look on our sin. This means that our sin causes us to be separated from God, our wonderful Maker.

Not only does our sin separate us from God here on earth, but it also leads to an eternal destiny far away from God, a place that has been prepared for the Devil and his helpers. Hell is a very real place of everlasting torment and agony. In Luke 16 Jesus tells a story about a rich man and a poor beggar who both died. When the poor man named Lazarus died, he was carried into heaven by angels. When the rich man died, he found himself tormented in hell. He cried out to Abraham in verse 24, saying, "...Father Abraham, have mercy on me, and send Lazarus, that he may dip the tip of his finger in water, and cool my tongue; for I am tormented in this flame."

Unfortunately, it was too late for this man. He had already rejected God's salvation while on earth and now had to suffer the consequences for all eternity.

When Jesus stretched out His arms of mercy on the cross and died for our sins, He was showing us just how much He loved us.

So is there any hope for us? Praise God, there is hope! The second part of Romans 6:23 tells us "...the gift of God is eternal life through Jesus Christ our Lord." There is a remedy for our sin problem, and that is the precious gift of eternal life.

John 3:16 is the most popular Bible verse of all time, and that's because it explains the plan of salvation prepared for us from the beginning of time. It reads, "For God so loved the world, that he gave his only begotten Son, that whosoever believeth in him should not perish, but have everlasting life."

There is only one way to obtain eternal life from God, and that is through His blessed Son, Jesus Christ. Romans 5:8 says, "But God commendeth his love toward us, in that, while we were yet sinners, Christ died for us." What wonderful news. When Jesus stretched out His arms of mercy on the cross and died for our sins, He was showing us just how much He loved us.

Allow me to say that Jesus loves you unconditionally, despite your sin. He wants to adopt you as His very own child and prepare a place for you in heaven. A place where there is no sin, sadness or suffering. Heaven is beautifully described in Revelation 7:16–17, which says:

> They shall hunger no more, neither thirst any more; neither shall the sun light on them, nor any heat. For the Lamb which is in the midst of the throne shall feed them, and shall lead them unto living fountains of waters: and God shall wipe away all tears from their eyes.

The Bible clearly explains how you can receive God's forgiveness from your sins and become His very own child. Romans 10 verses 9 and 13 state:

> That if thou shalt confess with thy mouth the Lord Jesus, and shalt believe in thine heart that God hath raised him from the dead, thou shalt be saved...For whosoever shall call upon the name of the Lord shall be saved.

God promises to give you eternal life if only you believe in Him and call upon His name.

I would like to invite you to ask Jesus to come into your life and save you from all your sins, to surrender your life to Jesus and start a new life as His child. He will come into your life and change you; that is His promise. God tells us in 1 John 1:9 that "If we confess our sins, he is faithful and just to forgive us our sins, and to cleanse us from all unrighteousness." The Lord wants to give you a fresh new start today. He wants to plant in you a desire to live for Him and give you the power to overcome sin. You can pray a simple prayer like this with all of your heart:

Lord, I know that I'm a sinner. I ask that You would forgive me.

Come into my heart and save me. Please make me Your own child and become Lord of my life today. Change me to be pleasing in Your sight. I want to live my life for You.

In Jesus's name I pray, Amen.

If you have just prayed this prayer, I encourage you to write down today's date below and seek out a Bible-believing church you can be part of. Today is officially the start of your new life in Christ.

Date _____

May God bless you, sister, and help you thrive in your new life in Christ!

Acknowledgments

To my Lord and Savior, Jesus Christ.
All glory goes to Thee, my Redeemer and my first love.

To my beloved husband, George.
Words can never express the depth of my love for you.
Thank you for always believing in me.

To my three treasures:
Bethany Joy, Samuel Alexander, and Marie-Therese.
May you always thrive in your relationship with Jesus.
I love you so much.

To my amazing dad, thank you for your Christlike
love all these years and the many happy memories
we have enjoyed together.

To my dear mother, thank you for leading me
to Christ as a little girl and never ceasing
to pray for me.

Notes

1. Linda Sabry, *A Single Pearl* (Sydney: Self-pub., 2011), 55.

2. Ann Omley, *"The Wise Man and the Foolish Man,"* (1948), Hymnary.org, https://hymnary.org/text/the_wise_man_built_his_house_upon_the_ro.

3. Elisabeth Elliot, *Quest for Love: True Stories of Passion and Purity* (Grand Rapids: Baker Publishing Group, 2002).

4. Shaunti Feldhahn and Robert Lewis, *The Life Ready Woman: Thriving in a Do-It-All World* (Nashville: B&H Publishing Group, 2011), 27.

5. Terrie Chappell, *The Choice Is Yours: Life Happens. Walking with God Is a Decision* (Lancaster, Calif.: Striving Together Publications, 2011), 5.

6. Elizabeth George, *A Woman's Guide to Making Right Choices* (Eugene, Ore.: Harvest House Publishers, 2012), 174.

7. Amy Carmichael, *Gold Cord: The Story of a Fellowship* (Fort Washington, Penna.: CLC Publications, 2002).

8. Elizabeth George, *A Woman After God's Own Heart* (Eugene, Ore.: Harvest House Publishers, 1997), 219–20.

9. Amy Carmichael, *Candles in the Dark: Letters of Hope and Encouragement* (Fort Washington, Penna.: CLC Publications, 2010).

10. J. Oswald Sanders, *Effective Faith* (United Kingdom, Kent: OMF Books, 1983).

11. Elizabeth George, *Powerful Promises for Every Woman: 12 Life-Changing Truths from Psalm 23* (Eugene, Ore.: Harvest House Publishers, 2003), 97–98.

12. Jim and Elizabeth George, *"How Do You Make God Your Priority?"* elizabethgeorge.com, https://elizabethgeorge.com/blogs/devos/how-do-you-make-god-your-priority.

13. Matthew Henry, *Matthew Henry's Commentary* (Grand Rapids: Zondervan, 1961), 908.

Printed in the United States
by Baker & Taylor Publisher Services